Practical Cases

in Special Education

for All Educators

Practical Cases
in Special Education
for All Educators

Mary Konya Weishaar
Southern Illinois University Edwardsville

Victoria Groves Scott
Southern Illinois University Edwardsville

Houghton Mifflin
Boston   New York

Editor-in-Chief: Patricia Coryell
Senior Sponsor: Sue Pulvermacher-Alt
Senior Development Editor: Lisa Mafrici
Senior Project Editor: Aileen M. Mason
Editorial Assistant: Susan Miscio
Senior Art & Design Coordinator: Jill Haber
Senior Photo Editor: Jennifer Meyer Dare
Senior Composition Buyer: Sarah Ambrose
Senior Manufacturing Coordinator: Marie Barnes
Marketing Manager: Laura McGinn

PHOTO CREDITS
Chapter 1: (top left) Bob Daemmrich/Bob Daemmrich Photography, (top right) Bob Daemmrich/PhotoEdit, Inc. (bottom) © Jeff Greenberg/Rainbow. *Chapter 2:* © Jeff Greenberg/Rainbow. *Chapter 3:* Bob Daemmrich/PhotoEdit, Inc. *Chapter 4:* Susan Van Etten/PhotoEdit, Inc. *Chapter 5:* Michael Newman/PhotoEdit, Inc. *Chapter 6:* Bob Daemmrich/Bob Daemmrich Photography. *Chapter 7:* Ellen Senisi/The Image Works. *Chapter 8:* Michael Newman/PhotoEdit, Inc. *Chapter 9:* Robin Sachs/PhotoEdit, Inc. *Chapter 10:* Williams Syndrome Association. *Chapter 11:* Courtesy of the Muscular Dystrophy Association. *Chapter 12:* Bob Daemmrich/PhotoEdit, Inc. *Chapter 13:* Bonnie Kamin/ PhotoEdit, Inc. *Chapter 14:* Laura Dwight/ PhotoEdit, Inc.

Printed in the U.S.A.

Library of Congress Control Number: 20055924691

ISBN: 0-618-37085-4

1 2 3 4 5 6 7 8 9-CRS-09 08 07 06 05

To my family—Paul, Mark, & Phil Weishaar
Pat & Joe Konya
for their support

MKW

To my father, Gayle Groves, who taught me
to enjoy each day to the fullest and
To all the families of children with disabilities
who have their own unique stories

VGS

BRIEF CONTENTS

Preface   xvii

CHAPTER 1   Using the Case Study Approach: Linking Theory and Practice   1

CHAPTER 2   Cases Involving Early Intervention   17

CHAPTER 3   Cases Involving Students Who Are Gifted and Talented   30

CHAPTER 4   Cases Involving Students with Mental Impairment and Developmental Disabilities   42

CHAPTER 5   Cases Involving Students with Learning Disabilities   56

CHAPTER 6   Cases Involving Students with Emotional and Behavior Disorders   68

CHAPTER 7   Cases Involving Students with Communication Disorders   82

CHAPTER 8   Cases Involving Students Who Are Deaf or Hard of Hearing   92

CHAPTER 9   Cases Involving Students with Visual Impairments   103

CHAPTER 10   Cases Involving Students with Multiple and Severe Disabilities   115

CHAPTER 11   Cases Involving Students with Physical Disabilities and Health Impairments   126

CHAPTER 12   Cases Involving Students with Autism and Pervasive Developmental Disorders   141

CHAPTER 13   Cases Involving Students with Traumatic Brain Injury   153

CHAPTER 14   Cases Involving Students with Attention Deficit Hyperactivity Disorder   164

Appendix   Individual Education Plan Drafting Activities and Templates   179

CONTENTS

Preface. . .xvii

Chapter 1 Using the Case Study Approach: Linking Theory and Practice   1

Background and Purpose of the Case Study Approach. 2
Using Your Experiences to Collect, Interpret, and Explain
  Circumstances Presented in the Case. 2
    Two Types of Cases. . .2
    Questions to Ponder. . .3
    Case Study Framework Questions. . .3
A Sample Case. 8
    Questions to Ponder. . .9
    Case Study Framework Questions. . .11
    Thinking Critically About the Case. . .11
Analyzing the Sample Case. 12
    Questions to Ponder. . .12
    Case Study Framework Questions. . .13
    Answers to Thinking Critically About the Case. . .14
Concluding Remarks. 15
    References. . .16

Chapter 2 Cases Involving Early Intervention   17

CASE 1: "Quinn". 18
Scot McCloud's Story. 18
    Questions to Ponder. . .20
Tori McCloud's Story. 20
Brenden McCloud's Story. 22
    Case Study Framework Questions. . .22
    Thinking Critically About the Case. . .23
    Activity. . .23
CASE 2: "Skylar". 24
Diagnostic Report. 24
    History of Presenting Complaint. . .24
    Social and Emotional Status. . .25

Assessments. . .25
Questions to Ponder. . .26
Summary. 26
Treatment Plan. 27
Case Study Framework Questions. . .28
Thinking Critically About the Case. . .28
Activity. . .28
References. . .29
Resources for Further Investigation. . .29

Chapter 3 Cases Involving Students Who Are Gifted and Talented　　**30**

CASE 1: "Carolyn". **31**
Questions to Ponder. . .32
Case Study Framework Questions. . .35
Thinking Critically About the Case. . .35
Activity. . .35
CASE 2: "Chancellor". **36**
Questions to Ponder. . .37
Case Study Framework Questions. . .40
Thinking Critically About the Case. . .40
Activity. . .40
Resources for Further Investigation. . .41

Chapter 4 Cases Involving Students with Mental Impairment and Developmental Disabilities　　**42**

CASE 1: "Sydney". **43**
Mr. Sears's Side. 43
Questions to Ponder. . .44
Mrs. Phelps's Side. 45
Case Study Framework Questions. . .46
Thinking Critically About the Case. . .47
Activity. . .47
CASE 2: "Miki". **48**
Questions to Ponder. . .50
Case Study Framework Questions. . .53
Thinking Critically About the Case. . .53

Activity. . .54
Resources for Further Investigation. . .54

**Chapter 5 Cases Involving Students
with Learning Disabilities   56**

CASE 1: "Benjamin". 57
Questions to Ponder. . .59
Case Study Framework Questions. . .61
Thinking Critically About the Case. . .61
Activity. . .61
CASE 2: "Duncan". 62
Questions to Ponder. . .64
Case Study Framework Questions. . .66
Thinking Critically About the Case. . .66
Activity. . .66
Resources for Further Investigation. . .67

**Chapter 6 Cases Involving Students with Emotional
and Behavior Disorders   68**

CASE 1: "Keesha". 69
Questions to Ponder. . .71
Case Study Framework Questions. . .72
Thinking Critically About the Case. . .73
Activity. . .73
CASE 2: "Adam". 74
Scenario 1. 74
Questions to Ponder. . .76
Scenario 2. 76
Case Study Framework Questions. . .78
Thinking Critically About the Case. . .78
Activity. . .79
Resources for Further Investigation. . .80

**Chapter 7 Cases Involving Students with Communication
Disorders   82**

CASE 1: "Kerim". 83
Questions to Ponder. . .84

Case Study Framework Questions. . .86
Thinking Critically About the Case. . .86
Activity. . .86

CASE 2: "Bradley". **87**
Questions to Ponder. . .88
Case Study Framework Questions. . .89
Thinking Critically About the Case. . .90
Activity. . .90
Resources for Further Investigation. . .91

Chapter 8 Cases Involving Students Who Are Deaf or Hard of Hearing   92

CASE 1: "James". **93**
Questions to Ponder. . .95
Case Study Framework Questions. . .97
Thinking Critically About the Case. . .97
Activity. . .97

CASE 2: "Kaleemah". **98**
Questions to Ponder. . .99
Case Study Framework Questions. . .101
Thinking Critically About the Case. . .101
Activity. . .102
Resources for Further Investigation. . .102

Chapter 9 Cases Involving Students with Visual Impairments   103

CASE 1: "Joey". **104**
Questions to Ponder. . .105
Case Study Framework Questions. . .107
Thinking Critically About the Case. . .108
Activity. . .108

CASE 2: "Sveta". **109**
Questions to Ponder. . .110
Case Study Framework Questions. . .113
Thinking Critically About the Case. . .114
Activity. . .114
Resources for Further Investigation. . .114

Chapter 10 Cases Involving Students with Multiple and Severe Disabilities   **115**

CASE 1: "Alexandrea"......116
  Questions to Ponder...117
  Case Study Framework Questions...119
  Thinking Critically About the Case...119
  Activity...119
CASE 2: "Tyvon"......120
  Questions to Ponder...121
  Case Study Framework Questions...124
  Thinking Critically About the Case...124
  Activity...124
  Resources for Further Investigation...125

Chapter 11 Cases Involving Students with Physical Disabilities and Health Impairments   **126**

CASE 1: "Mark"......127
  Questions to Ponder...129
  Case Study Framework Questions...130
  Thinking Critically About the Case...130
  Activity...130
CASE 2: "Kate"......131
  Questions to Ponder...132
New IEP...138
  Case Study Framework Questions...139
  Thinking Critically About the Case...140
  Activity...140
  Resources for Further Investigation...140

Chapter 12 Cases Involving Students with Autism and Pervasive Developmental Disorders   **141**

CASE 1: "Max"......142
A Teacher's Reflections......142
  Questions to Ponder...144
  Case Study Framework Questions...145
  Thinking Critically About the Case...146
  Activity...146

CASE 2: "Rashmi". **147**
Questions to Ponder. . .*149*
Functions of Behavior. 149
Case Study Framework Questions. . .*151*
Thinking Critically About the Case. . .*151*
Activity. . .*151*
Resources for Further Investigation. . .*152*

Chapter 13 Cases Involving Students with Traumatic Brain Injury   153

CASE 1: "Gustavo". **154**
Questions to Ponder. . .*155*
Case Study Framework Questions. . .*157*
Thinking Critically About the Case. . .*157*
Activity. . .*158*
CASE 2: "Andrew". **159**
Questions to Ponder. . .*160*
Case Study Framework Questions. . .*162*
Thinking Critically About the Case. . .*162*
Activity. . .*163*
Resources for Further Investigation. . .*163*

Chapter 14 Cases Involving Students with Attention Deficit Hyperactivity Disorder   164

CASE 1: "John". **165**
Questions to Ponder. . .*167*
Case Study Framework Questions. . .*168*
Thinking Critically About the Case. . .*168*
Activity. . .*168*
CASE 2: "Jerry". **169**
Jerry. . .169
Questions to Ponder. . .*170*
Mrs. Meuth. . .170
Mrs. Basco. . .171
Mr. Kova. . .172

Case Study Framework Questions. . .176
Thinking Critically About the Case. . .177
Activity. . .177
Resources for Further Investigation. . .178

APPENDIX: Individual Education Plan Drafting Activities
and Templates. 179

PREFACE

How would you, as a general education teacher, special education teacher, or administrator, handle the following scenarios?

Michael, seven years old, has attention deficit disorder and has been placed in a general education second-grade classroom. Lately, he has been constantly fidgeting, blurting out answers, grabbing pencils from other students, and getting up without raising his hand. His teacher, who has thirty students in her class, said, "He just never listens or does what he's supposed to do. When he misbehaves, the other twenty-nine students miss out on learning. If he needs special attention, then he should be put in special education. They can probably handle him better."

Jamil is a fifteen-year-old student with learning disabilities in Mr. James's social studies class. At Jamil's individual education plan meeting last spring, it was determined that Jamil needed to have someone read social studies tests aloud to him. This year in class, Jamil is failing, in part because no one carried out this accommodation. When the learning disabilities teacher talked with Mr. James in October about the needed accommodation, Mr. James said, "I see 180 students every day! If any students in special education are placed in my classes, they must have the skills to succeed or they shouldn't be there. I don't have time to arrange to have tests read aloud to one student."

The superintendent of schools spoke to the special education administrator in her office. She said, "Our test scores in reading declined again this past year, partly because of students in special education taking the test. These students are pulling our test scores down. Isn't there any way they can be excluded from taking the reading test? Shouldn't they be assessed using specialized tests?"

These scenarios illustrate some of the problems and concerns that persist in special education and general education. Some problems arise from students with disabilities who receive part or most of their education in the general education classroom. In the first scenario, the teacher is clearly frustrated about how she can meet the needs of a child who has attention deficit disorder. With 30 students, it may seem logical for the teacher to want this child "placed" in special education. In the second scenario, the high school teacher is too overwhelmed to provide special accommodations for 1 student when he teaches 180 students every day. In the third scenario, a superintendent is worried about the effects of special students taking required achievement tests and the resulting public perception. All three scenarios raise questions about the working relationship between general educators and special educators.

It is no longer enough to say that public schools have "opened their doors" to students with disabilities and that the schools' responsibilities are therefore met. It is no longer relevant to suggest that general education has one set of expectations and special education has another. If all children are to succeed and learn in today's public schools, the relationship between general and special educators must be a positive one and all educators must become informed about their responsibilities to all children. All educators are responsible for the outcomes and success of all children, whether in general education or special education.

How to Use This Text

This text uses the case study approach to show how general educators can and should become active participants in the education of children who have disabilities. The case studies emphasize the following factors:

1. Basic principles of the Individuals with Disabilities Education Improvement Act (parent participation, due process, individualized education plan, nondiscriminatory evaluation, zero reject/child find, least restrictive environment)

2. Foundations of legislation, like No Child Left Behind, that deal with accountability and shared responsibility for the education of all children

3. Additional important issues (response to intervention, prereferral process, strengths-based planning) and disabilities (e.g., attention deficit hyperactivity disorder, autism spectrum disorder) that are not typically addressed in a casebook

We intend this text to be used as a supplement to a comprehensive survey or advanced text on characteristics of students with disabilities or as the main text for someone using a case-based approach and focusing on applications. Undergraduate students often take a survey course focusing on characteristics of students with disabilities, and graduate students sometimes take advanced courses on this subject. This text provides both undergraduate and graduate students with much needed practical applications that show how general and special educators must work together and become involved in the education of all children. A discussion of these case studies will narrow the gap between learning about characteristics of children with disabilities and knowing how to work with real children who have those disabilities in a school.

Description and Organization of the Cases

The case studies in this text are based on actual situations. However, names and other identifying information, as well as some facts, have been changed. In some instances the cases are embellished to make a point, but they essentially represent reality. Some cases are examples of best practice on the part of educators, and others show less-than-best practice. We believe that undergraduate and graduate students can learn a great deal from both situations.

Chapter 1, "Using the Case Study Approach: Linking Theory and Practice," discusses how to use a case study to develop one's critical thinking skills. A sample case is also discussed and analyzed.

The next thirteen chapters contain case studies that illustrate various disabilities. Throughout the text, there is a balance of early childhood (ages 3–5), elementary (grades K–5), middle school (grades 6–8), and high school (grades 9–12) cases. We firmly believe that services for students with disabilities should be individually determined based on student need and not on disability category. However, it is also understood that many university courses are organized around special education categories. Therefore, we attempt to align the case chapters with typical survey texts. The chapters cover early intervention (Chapter 2), gifted and talented students (Chapter 3), mental impairment and developmental disabilities (Chapter 4), learning disabilities (Chapter 5), emotional and behavior disorders (Chapter 6), communication disorders (Chapter 7), students who are deaf or hard of hearing (Chapter 8), visual impairments (Chapter 9), multiple and severe disabilities (Chapter 10), physical disabilities and health impairments (Chapter 11), autism spectrum disorder (Chapter 12), traumatic brain injury (Chapter 13), and attention deficit hyperactivity disorder (Chapter 14).

Special Features and Pedagogy

Each chapter contains two cases that address different situations, ages, student characteristics, forms of cultural identification, and socioeconomic status. Each case study is built around a framework to help the reader organize and analyze the important aspects of the case.

Questions to Ponder

These questions are located in the middle of each case to help the reader focus on who is telling the story, connect his or her personal background and experience with the case issues, and identify the facts and opinions presented.

Case Study Framework Questions

The questions that follow each case assist the reader with in-depth analysis (see Chapter 1 for a discussion of these questions). The questions include

1. What makes this a contemplation (and/or examplar) case?

2. How do emotions influence behaviors in the main characters?

3. How is factual information consistent with professional literature?

4. Are issues oversimplified? Why?

5. Are people stereotyped? How?

6. Discuss teacher dispositions that facilitate or could become a barrier to working with the student discussed in the case (i.e., self-reflection, tolerance for others, collaboration, multiple perspectives, sound ethical judgment, motivation to work with students with a variety of needs, capacity for advocacy).

Thinking Critically About the Case

Following the case study questions are more detailed questions to help the reader think critically about the case and to address the specific issues that have been raised; these questions often revolve around legal and ethical issues.

Activity

An active learning activity is placed at the end of each case to further the reader's critical thinking skills and knowledge.

Resources for Further Investigation

At the end of each chapter, a list of current works of literature and online resources is included to enhance the reader's further exploration of the disability.

Appendix: Individual Education Plan Drafting Activities and Templates

At the end of the book, an activity with blank Individual Education Plan (IEP) worksheets is included that allows a cohort group of students to reflect on any case study in the book, role-play an IEP meeting, and make important decisions related to the special education services to be provided, as well as to transitions, goals, and state and local assessments.

It is important to note that questions posed in this text sometimes do not have a right or wrong answer. It is therefore imperative to discuss the questions thoroughly and to provide answers that are supported with data. This discussion is essential to developing critical thinking skills, dispositions, and problem-solving skills. We have provided a number of sample responses for instructors (on the instructor website at **http://college.hmco.com/education**) to help explain why we ask particular questions. We hope such potential answers offer another useful perspective. In addition to the sample case responses, the accompanying textbook website offers additional resources, including Houghton Mifflin Video Cases, live weblinks from the text, and the IEP drafting activities and templates from the appendix.

Acknowledgments

We wish to thank Sue Pulvermacher-Alt, Lisa Mafrici, and Beth Kaufman for their support in developing this text and for their excellent suggestions on improving it. We also appreciate the helpful feedback from our field reviewers:

Teresa D. Bunsen, University of Alaska

J'Anne Ellsworth, Northern Arizona University

Michelle Erklenz-Watts, St. John Fisher College

Christine J. Evans, Simmons College

Jane M. Hardin, Simmons College

Kent Jackson, Indiana University of Pennsylvania

Karen L. Kelly, Colorado Department of Education

Timothy Lillie, The University of Akron

Carol A. Long, Winona State University

Joan Marshall, SUNY Oneonta

Paul McKnab, Emporia State University

Kathlyn Parker, Eastern Michigan University

Debra P. Price, Sam Houston State University

Eileen Dugan Sabbatino, Saint Joseph's University

Saundra N. Shorter, Fayetteville State University

Jane M. Williams, University of Nevada, Las Vegas

Wendy Woods, Kent State University

We also wish to thank Dr. Elliott Lessen, Dean, School of Education, Southern Illinois University Edwardsville and Dr. Bill Searcy, Chairperson, Department of Special Education and Communication Disorders, Southern Illinois University Edwardsville for their support of our work.

MKW
VGS

Chapter 1

Using the Case Study Approach: Linking Theory and Practice

Background and Purpose of the Case Study Approach

The use of case studies in teacher education programs can be traced back to the 1920s, when Anderson, Barr, and Bush published *Visiting the Teacher at Work: Case Studies of Directed Teaching.* The case study method of instruction has also been used in the fields of law, medicine, business, and engineering. However, within the last several years, cases have "come into their own in the area of teacher preparation" (Kuntz & Hessler, 1998, p. 4). Cases are developed from typical and recurrent problems encountered by practitioners in the field. In describing a situation, case narratives engage the reader and enable him or her to vicariously participate in a teacher's experience. The cases in this text are based on true situations, but the names and certain details have been changed to protect privacy or to emphasize a certain point. They are designed to facilitate active involvement and to help the practitioner link theory to practice.

More specifically, as Kuntz and Hessler (1998) outline, case studies are designed to stimulate thinking and to encourage professionals in education to

- Employ higher-order thinking skills
- Generalize learning to the classroom, school, and wider community
- Question assumptions underlying the theories presented
- Draw on self-analysis skills
- Realize the judgmental and complex nature of teaching
- Apply knowledge of issues in today's society

Using Your Experiences to Collect, Interpret, and Explain Circumstances Presented in the Case

Two Types of Cases

The use of different types of cases leads to a deeper understanding of complex issues (Jay, 2004). The cases in this book tend to fall into two categories (Merseth, 1996):

- *Exemplar cases* that show best practice
- *Contemplation cases* that provide opportunity to practice analysis and assimilate different perspectives

Identifying which kind of case you are reading helps you understand its intention and its key ideas. We discuss this issue in more detail in relation to the case study framework questions listed later.

Questions to Ponder

In the middle of each case the text asks you to stop and ponder certain basic questions:

- Whose story is this?
- What is my background or previous experience with the issues presented in this case?
- What facts are presented?
- What opinions are presented?

Many of the cases will be written from the perspective of a particular person. Some will include multiple perspectives. As the reader, you should be able to identify the person telling the story and the role of that character in the story. Some cases might be written from the perspective of the person with the disability, some from the parent's perspective, and some from the general educator or special educator's perspective.

As you read, you should also think about your knowledge in the particular area being discussed. For example, if the case is in the section on severe or multiple disabilities, you should think about your content knowledge and personal knowledge in that field. What professional knowledge have you gained from courses and readings, and what experiences have you had with persons with that type of disability?

Next you need to look for the facts presented in the case, usually presented in the description of the characters. Facts include the age of the character and the disability diagnosis; they also include the events of the case. Opinions may be more difficult to identify. The following statements express opinions: "Attending Individualized Educational Program meetings is the job of the special educator and a waste of time for the general educator," "Students with disabilities deserve to be placed in the best general education classes," or "I wouldn't know what to do in the classroom with a student who is blind." You should also identify how closely your own opinions match those of the characters. Finally, you should try to determine why you might hold that opinion.

Case Study Framework Questions

After you read each case, you are asked to reflect on six basic questions that are relevant to every case. They are discussed in detail next.

1. *What makes this a contemplation (and/or exemplar) case?* To understand and analyze a particular situation, it is useful to determine what actions are best practice and what are less than best practice. In some real-life cases, the decisions made and the actions taken are less than best practice, but the authors think teachers learn as much from these cases as they do from model or exemplar cases.

   An exemplar case tends to present sound knowledge of theory or practice relating to students with disabilities. The educational system described seems idealistic. The student's needs are met within the least restrictive environment with maximum parent participation. The case may seem to emphasize collaborative teamwork and problem solving, and the teachers and professionals will appear to go out of their way to accommodate the student and his or her family and to attempt to improve the student's academic skills and quality of life. You will find professionals who are conscious of people-first language and ethical conduct. In these cases, the authors have decided to portray the best of education and effective teaching. Additionally, the cases meet all requirements and legal mandates set forth by the Individuals with Disabilities Education Improvement Act of 2004 (IDEA) and No Child Left Behind Act (NCLB).

   In contemplation cases, on the other hand, there may be no easy solution. Multiple problems and multiple perspectives may be presented. These cases tend to be "messy." They present complicated situations and require the reader to identify and analyze the situation presented. Thus, in contemplation cases there may be no right answer; instead, there may be several adequate solutions, depending on one's viewpoint. These cases may not represent best or recommended practice in education. They may also violate the legal requirements expressed in IDEA or NCLB.

   Both types of cases may ask for personal reflection. In discussing a case, you may be asked to make a connection to your current practices with questions like "Have you ever seen this done in practice?" or "Have you worked with a family like this one?" You may also be asked to make a personal reflection using your current belief system. In this instance, you may be asked, "How would you feel in this situation?" or "What would you do in this situation?"

2. *How do emotions influence behaviors in the main characters?* Until they gain experience with a particular disability, many teachers believe that working with students with that disability will be difficult. Often this is due to their fear. They express fear that they won't know what to do with the student or that they will do something wrong. Other emotions to look for are frustration,

despair, grief, anger, satisfaction, pride, and excitement. Also examine how these emotions influence the behavior of the characters in the story. For example, parents in the grief process after their child has been diagnosed with a disability might appear to be uninterested in their child's schooling, but in fact the grief is too consuming to allow them to act. They might need time to process the grief they feel before they are able to participate in the education program.

It is always helpful to identify those instances when decisions are based on emotion rather than rational thinking. If teachers can identify their emotions and understand how they influence their behaviors, they might be able to address difficult situations in a more positive manner before they become problematic.

3. *How is the factual information consistent with current professional literature?* You should also critically examine the cases for misinformation. Often parents, as well as professionals, hold ideas that are not consistent with what is stated in the professional literature. Although there is no research to support the notion that sugar causes children to be overactive, many teachers and parents believe this idea. Additionally, current research suggests that auditory processing difficulties are more prevalent than visual processing difficulties in students with dyslexia. However, many parents and teachers still believe that a child labeled dyslexic "sees things backward," even though this is very rare. To help you identify misinformation, you can use current textbooks or professional journal articles. You should compare the information from these professional sources to the ideas held by characters in the case.

4. *Are issues oversimplified? If so, how?* Oversimplifications are easily made when one's background knowledge lacks depth and breadth. It is essential to identify them because hypotheses that are built on oversimplifications generally lead to faulty conclusions. For instance, team members who assume that once students with a disability are placed in special education they will no longer have problems in school may be surprised when a student continues to experience difficulties. Likewise, if a teacher states that all children with attention deficit hyperactivity disorder should take Ritalin, this is an oversimplification, because medication is not appropriate for all children with this disability. Identifying the oversimplifications in each case can help you reduce the number of faulty conclusions you might make.

5. *Are people stereotyped? If so, how?* Stereotypes may be identified by analyzing the language used by the characters in each case. Any time

characters use language other than "people-first" language, they perpetuate a stereotype. Children are not "autistic children," "Down's kids," or "crippled students." They are *children, kids,* and *students* first. They should be described as persons *with* a particular disability or diagnosis.

Other stereotypes are related to generalizations about groups of individuals. For example, if an administrator states that all children with Down syndrome should be placed in separate special education classes, the administrator is acting on a stereotype, because not all children with Down syndrome have the same abilities. Stereotypes can also be positive or negative. Both are damaging because they prejudge individuals based on their perceived membership in a particular group or category. Examples of negative stereotypes might include "Students with learning disabilities are generally lazy and unmotivated" and "If parents would discipline their child better he/she wouldn't have attention deficit hyperactivity disorder." Examples of positive stereotypes would be "All special education teachers are patient" and "Children with cognitive delays are sweet, loving, and well behaved." Although those are nice opinions, they certainly aren't true for all special education teachers or all children with cognitive delays. It is useful to identify stereotypes so that appropriate decisions can be made and respect for the individual can be maintained.

6. *Discuss teacher dispositions that facilitate or could become a barrier to working with the student discussed in the case.* Dispositions are those attitudes that professionals in the field of education have identified as being essential in successful interactions with parents and students. They are the keys to success in teaching. Dispositions are often difficult to measure. In fact, many teacher education programs struggle with dispositions on a daily basis. It's easy to grade students or practitioners on lesson plan development but difficult to evaluate their commitment to continued learning. When evaluating dispositions during cases, you must focus on self-reflection. Examine your own dispositions by asking if your solution to this problem or analysis of this case shows (1) a respect for diversity and tolerance for others, (2) a willingness to collaborate and learn from others, (3) the ability to look at situations from others points of view, (4) sound ethical judgment, (5) motivation to work with students with a variety of needs, and (6) the capability to advocate for students with disabilities and their families.

The following table lists all the case parts we have been discussing. You can copy this list and use one copy for each case, entering information for the specific case you are dealing with on the right. By answering the questions, you will be able to thoroughly analyze important aspects of each case. The questions and answers also provide a framework for discussion in small groups within the university classroom.

Case Study Characteristics	Particular Case

Case Categories
  • Exemplar
  • Contemplation	

Questions to Ponder
  • Whose story is this?
  • What is my background or previous experience with the issues presented in this case?
  • What facts are presented?
  • What opinions are presented?	

Case Study Framework Questions
  • What makes this a contemplation/exemplar case?
  • How do emotions influence behaviors in the main characters?
  • How is factual information consistent with current professional literature?
  • Are issues oversimplified? If so, how?
  • Are people stereotyped? If so, how?
  • Discuss teacher dispositions that facilitate or could become a barrier to working with the student discussed in the case.	

Dispositions
  • Self-reflection
  • Tolerance for others
  • Collaboration
  • Multiple perspectives
  • Sound ethical judgment
  • Motivation to work with students with a variety of needs
  • Capacity for advocacy	

Lastly, the text offers some questions that have to do with the specific case, titled "Thinking Critically About the Case." The questions in this section will require to you summarize information presented in the case or make evaluations about the appropriateness of the actions taken. You may also be asked to give your opinion and to support your opinion with facts related to the case.

A Sample Case

Now that you have some basic understanding of the case study approach to teacher education, it's time to practice. The following minicase will give you the chance to engage in some case study analysis.

"Kyler"

Type of Case: **Contemplation**

Age Level: **Elementary School**

Characters

Kyler Edmon, a five-year-old girl with a language delay

Mr. and Mrs. Edmon, Kyler's parents

Linda Pape, kindergarten teacher at Meadowbrook Elementary

Virginia Baker, Special Education Administrator for District 134

I've attended a lot of Individualized Education Program (IEP) meetings in the twenty years that I've been teaching, but this one felt adversarial, which is very unusual for kindergarten. Usually the parents I work with are worried their child won't fit in or his or her needs won't be met, and I feel like it's my job as the general kindergarten teacher to show a positive attitude and a willingness to work with their child. By the end of most meetings, we all feel like a team. That's one of my favorite parts of working with children with disabilities. It's easy to teach a bright, well-behaved child, with no special needs. It takes a good teacher to work with children with special needs.

At first, I dreaded having children with disabilities in my class. I remember the summer I found out I would have a student with Down syndrome in my class. She was my first "included" student, and I didn't feel ready. I have to admit that I didn't want her, but she changed my view of children. She was loving, stubborn, affectionate, and excited about everything we did. She was one of my best students that year! In fact, she still comes to visit me occasionally, even though she just turned thirteen.

When I found out Kyler would be in my kindergarten class next year I was eager to attend the IEP and to make a plan to work with Kyler. I had heard about Kyler from her preschool teachers, so I already had a lot of information about Kyler. She had attended the early childhood special education preschool program in the district for two years and was ready to go to kindergarten. Her family lived on a farm just outside of town. Kyler's mother, Mrs. Edmon, was a registered nurse and worked at the hospital. Her father, Mr. Edmon, was a farmer. Kyler was a small girl with big brown eyes and brown curly hair. She didn't start to speak until she was well past three. At five, she had some basic signs for common words, and spoke in two word sentences. Her play was very delayed, and she had some unusual behaviors. Kyler rarely made eye contact. She tended to "organize her toys" instead of play with them; for example, she sorted all her dolls by the colors they wore. She became very upset when she was asked to do anything that she wasn't interested in at the time. She could spend hours swinging and refused to come inside. She hated things that were sticky and wouldn't play with clay or sand. On the other hand, Kyler could write her first and last name, knew all the letters in the alphabet, and could do pages of basic addition and subtraction sheets with very few errors.

▶▶ Questions to Ponder

▶ Whose story is this?

▶ What is my background or previous experience with the issues presented in this case?

▶ What facts are presented?

▶ What opinions are presented?

I was prepared to work with the special education teacher and make my classroom welcoming to Kyler and her parents, but her parents wanted her to remain at the early childhood center for another year. Although the psychologist reported that he saw tendencies of a pervasive developmental disorder, Kyler's only diagnosis was a language delay. Mrs. Edmond believed that Kyler would "grow out of her language problems" with a little more time. That's why they wanted to delay the start of kindergarten until Kyler was six, which was not that unusual. I often have children, with no special needs, who start kindergarten soon after their sixth birthday.

I could tell, after thirty minutes into the IEP meeting, that the teachers at the early childhood center didn't want this little girl. They seemed to want to force the parents into accepting that their child had autism and would never be normal. The underlying tone was that they had served Kyler at the early childhood center for two years and it was time for her to move to elementary school.

I've known Virginia Baker, the special education administrator for the early childhood program, for years. That happens when you work in a small district with someone for over fifteen years. Virginia had a reputation for not standing her ground with her teachers and being pushed around during meetings. I had heard gossip about the strong-willed early childhood teachers who wouldn't attend staff meetings or make home visits as the district required. But even knowing that there were problems at the early childhood center, I wasn't prepared for that meeting.

After the special education teachers and speech and language pathologists each talked about their programs, the goals, and the benchmarks, Virginia began to talk. She explained that the elementary school would provide a more inclusive environment for Kyler to be with children without disabilities. Mr. and Mrs. Edmon didn't see this as a positive. They were worried that Kyler's language and social delays would make her "stick out" in the class. They didn't want her to be left out, because she didn't interact well with other children. I explained that it was my job to teach the children how to get along and how to work with fellow classmates. Mrs. Edmon said that she believed Kyler's language and play would develop faster in a more structured environment, like the early childhood center, which had only ten children per teacher and a teacher's assistant. Kyler's parents also wanted more direct speech and language services. Mrs. Edmon thought this would be easier to get at the early childhood center, because they had their own speech and language pathologist. At the elementary school, the speech and language pathologist served students in two schools with over three hundred children in each building. Both Mr. and Mrs. Edmon felt that after a year Kyler would be better equipped to handle the demands of a kindergarten room and be ready to be included more in the general kindergarten class.

It was then that Virginia looked at the Edmons and said, "Of course the decision is up to you, but I want you to consider the burden that you are placing on the early childhood center. If every child that needed a more structured environment stayed at the early childhood center for another year, then what would we do? We already have six new children starting in the fall. Two of the children have significant needs. We don't have the staff to sufficiently address Kyler's needs in this class, and the special education teacher's caseload at the elementary school is very low for next year."

I just looked at her. Did she realize what she had said? In essence, she told the whole team that the district was here to serve the teachers, not the children. What really mattered was how the staff was impacted, NOT how the child was educated. I could understand the argument that Kyler needed to be with typically developing peers, or that she needed more academic instruction, since her reading and math skills seemed to be even above kindergarten level, but I did not believe that she was a burden to the system. If not illegal, this statement was an affront to every principle set forth in the Individuals with Disabilities Education Improvement Act 2004 (IDEA).

Case Study Framework Questions

1. What makes this a contemplation case?
2. How do emotions influence behaviors in the main characters?
3. How is the factual information consistent with current professional literature?
4. Are issues oversimplified? If so, how?
5. Are people stereotyped? If so, how?
6. Discuss teacher dispositions that facilitate or could become a barrier to working with the student discussed in the case (i.e., self-reflection, tolerance for others, collaboration, multiple perspectives, sound ethical judgment, motivation to work with students with a variety of needs, capacity for advocacy).

Thinking Critically About the Case

1. What is Kyler's diagnosis?
2. Where do you believe Kyler would best be served?
3. If you were in Linda Pape's position, what would you say to Virginia Baker?
4. Was Virginia Baker's statement illegal? Why or why not?
5. What other professionals should be involved, and what should they be doing?

Analyzing the Sample Case

The Appendix at the end of this book provides a handy activity and several sample IEP templates that you can use to build a mock IEP for Kyler. In the forms provided, you will be asked to identify Kyler's current levels of performance, general education modifications, transition plan to elementary school, and participation in state and local assessments.

Using the Case Study Framework, let's analyze this case. We will start with the questions in the middle of the case under the title "Questions to Ponder."

Questions to Ponder

- Whose story is this?

This is Linda Pape's story, the general education kindergarten teacher.

- What is my background or previous experience with the issues presented in this case?

What do you know about early childhood special education and transition to kindergarten? What do you know about language delays and pervasive developmental disorder? What do you know about the Individuals with Disabilities Education Act? What experiences do you have that might relate to this case?

- What facts are presented?
  - Kyler is a five-year-old girl diagnosed as having a language delay.
  - She lives with her parents on a farm.
  - Kyler didn't talk until she was three. She now speaks in two-word utterances and uses simple sign language. She can write her first and last name, knows all the letters in the alphabet, and can do basic addition and subtraction.
  - Klyer's parents want her to stay at the early childhood center for another year.
  - Linda Pape is looking forward to working with Kyler and her parents.
- What opinions are presented?
  - Linda Pape enjoys working with students with special needs.
  - Mrs. Edmon believes that Kyler will "grow out" of her disability.
  - Mr. and Mrs. Edmon believe that Kyler will develop skills within the next year that will better prepare her to be included in a general kindergarten class.

- Virginia Baker believes that allowing Kyler to remain at the early childhood center will place a burden on the teaching staff and the system.

Case Study Framework Questions

Next, let's look at the questions at the end of the case.

- What makes this a contemplation case?

In this case, the general education teacher represents an exemplar example, and the case is a contemplation case. Although Linda Pape represents an effective teacher, Virginia Baker makes statements at the IEP meeting that would necessitate an analysis of the situation. Additionally, the disagreement about the appropriate placement has pros and cons for each side, which makes the case a "messy" case with several adequate solutions.

This case also requires personal reflection, because two of the questions asked at the end of the case require you to give your opinion. You are asked to make a judgment about where Kyler would be best served, and what you would do in the situation. To help you prepare your answer, you are asked to consider the following questions:

- How do emotions influence behaviors in the main characters?
  - The Edmons may be afraid to let Kyler attend elementary school.
  - Linda Pape is upset about the statement of Kyler being a "burden to the system." The case doesn't say, but she may allow her emotions to influence her response to Virginia Baker.
- How is the factual information consistent with current professional literature?

To answer this question, you can compare the case information with information from your special education textbook or additional texts or journal articles. For this case, the answer would be yes. Children with diagnosed disabilities are eligible for special education services under IDEA at the age of three. These services are often offered in early childhood programs administered by the local school district. It is also common for children with forms of pervasive developmental disorder to be given the diagnosis of language delayed until later. This is especially true for those children with milder characteristics. If Kyler does have a form of pervasive developmental disorder, she may receive special education services under the category of developmental delay until the age of nine. It is also common to include children with disabilities in general education classes as early as possible. Children need to be taught how to work in inclusive environments early on before they learn stereotypes and prejudices about those who are different.

• Are issues oversimplified?

No, it appears that everyone on the team realizes that Kyler is going to need ongoing support. However, Kyler's parents may be underestimating the severity and the lifelong nature of their child's disability. On the other hand, it is important for professionals to validate the parents' feelings in a realistic fashion. They may want to say it is unlikely that Kyler will "grow out of her language problems." However, it is not impossible. If parents give up hope for their child's future, then so will everyone else. The field of education is filled with examples of children who "grew out of something." In fact, some of our most famous inventors and leaders struggled with language, academics, and social skills. Professionals may be the experts in the field of education, but parents are the experts about their child.

• Are people stereotyped?
  • No, Linda Pape told this story using consistent people-first language.
  • No assumptions were made about individuals in the case based on their affiliation with a group. The characters in the case appeared to evaluate each other on an individual basis instead of according to perceptions about groups or categories.
• Discuss teacher dispositions that facilitate or could become a barrier to working with the student discussed in the case.

This last framework question makes you better equipped to answer the next set of questions, "Thinking Critically About the Case."It asks you to become aware of your dispositions. Do you have a respect for everyone concerned? Are you willing to listen to others' ideas on the case and assimilate their perceptions into your answers? Are you showing sound, ethical judgment? Do you think that you could be a good advocate for this case? The answer to these questions may be difficult to articulate, but only by being aware of your own dispositions can you change any attitudes that may become barriers to teaching successfully and working with students with special needs and their families.

Answers to Thinking Critically About the Case

1. *What is Kyler's diagnosis?* Kyler's only diagnosis is a language delay, however, the psychologist did note that he saw tendencies associated with a pervasive developmental disorder.

2. *Where do you believe Kyler would best be served?* Based on Kyler's parents' strong feelings that Kyler should remain in the early childhood special education setting, it is probably best to leave Kyler in that placement for another year. Her age makes her still eligible for

this placement. Additionally, the fact that a full-time speech/language pathologist is assigned to the early childhood program might ensure that Kyler has more opportunity for speech and language services. No matter where the placement, the decision should NEVER be based on what the system has to offer or what the district can afford to supply. All placement decisions should be based on a consensus of what is most appropriate for the child.

3. *If you were in Linda Pape's position, what would you say to Virginia Baker?* It would be appropriate for Linda Pape to respond by reminding the team that they are there to decide what is best for Kyler not for the early childhood center. Linda should also make it clear that Kyler is not a burden.

4. *Was Virginia Baker's statement illegal? Why or why not?* Yes, there is federal law that protects the rights of children with disabilities to free and appropriate public education. The law ensures students that reasonable placement decisions will be made based on the child's needs and not funding, staffing, or other administrative issues.

5. *What other professionals should be involved, and what should they be doing?* In addition to the parents, kindergarten teacher, and administrator, both the early childhood and elementary special education teachers and speech/language pathologists should attend the meeting. It was unclear if all of these individuals were present. The kindergarten special education teacher and speech/language pathologist could talk about the services Kyler could get through special education and explain how they would collaborate with Linda Pape to provide Kyler with appropriate services. Additionally, a school psychologist and/or behavior consultant might be appropriate to offer suggestions on how to provide positive behavior supports for Kyler's behavior. The parents might want to ask a parent advocate to attend the meeting to advise them on their rights and legal issues.

Concluding Remarks

The following cases are organized in chapters by disability categories. Each chapter is arranged in the following manner: (1) case title, (2) age level, (3) characters, (4) case study, (5) questions to ponder during reading, (6) case study framework questions, and (7) critical thinking questions. Each case contains both framework and critical thinking questions, and they are designed to be used selectively; it is not necessary to answer all of them. On the inside front cover of this book, you will find a handy matrix listing the type of case and the age level categories.

As you practice analyzing cases, you should be able to increase your knowledge of issues in special education and hone your problem-solving skills. You should be encouraged to discuss your opinions honestly and be open to suggestions from others. Through these discussions, you will learn to critically reflect on key theories and practices in special education and also learn to link the two together.

REFERENCES

Anderson, C. J., Barr, A. S., & Bush, M. G. (1925). *Visiting the teacher at work: Case studies of direct teaching.* New York: Appleton.

Jay, J. K. (2004). Variations on the use of cases in social work and teacher education. *Journal of Curriculum Studies, 36*(1), 35–39.

Kuntz, S., & Hessler, A. (1998). *Bridging the gap between theory and practice: Fostering active learning through the case study method* (Report No. SPO37985). Washington, DC: Association of American Colleges and Universities. (ERIC Document Reproduction Service No. ED420626)

Merseth, K. K. (1996). Cases and case methods in teacher education. In J. Sikula (Ed.), *Handbook of research on teacher education* (pp. 722–744). New York: Macmillan.

Chapter 2

Cases Involving Early Intervention

CASE 1 "Quinn"

Type of Case: Contemplation
Age Level: Early Childhood

Characters

Quinn McCloud, four-year-one-month-old boy diagnosed
  with a language delay

Tori McCloud, Quinn's mother

Scot McCloud, Quinn's father

Brenden McCloud, Quinn's eight-year-old brother

Scot McCloud's Story

It was late in the afternoon, toward the middle of April, when Tori and
I were experiencing an emergency c-section with the delivery of our
second son Quinn. The c-section was completed without any apparent
incidence, but sometimes what you can't physically see with your own
eyes can be the most dangerous.

As time went by, Tori and I noticed Quinn was having trouble
standing and walking. He continuously tried to stand on his toes. Over
the next few months it became alarming, and even though the pediatrician wasn't concerned, we took him to see a specialist when he was
fifteen months old.

It was explained to us that Quinn either had a mild form of cerebral
palsy, or he was experiencing what the neurologist termed, "congenital
toe walking." Whatever the case was, Quinn was to wear a brace on his
right foot for six months to possibly two years.

As we left the specialist's office, I asked Tori to explain the term
cerebral palsy. I knew Tori, being a special educator and professor, would
have almost as much information as the doctor. She explained that
cerebral palsy was caused by brain damage, probably resulting from the
emergency c-section. It would affect Quinn's life physically and could
cause other developmental delays as well. Needless to say, I hoped Quinn
had congenital toe walking.

We had just moved to a new state, and we knew Quinn was going to
require daily physical therapy. Tori had just taken a position at a state

university, so we were unsure how we would balance Quinn's needs with two full-time jobs. We decided it would be best for me to become a stay-at-home dad. I started working with Quinn two to three hours a day. We took Quinn to physical therapy, and I learned the stretching techniques to do at home. I tried to balance stretching activities with fun movement exercises like stair climbing and push toys. Quinn was fitted for a brace, and he wore it 24 hours a day. He kept the brace on continuously for three months. The only time we took it off was for bath time. Quinn really didn't mind the brace, and within two weeks he could stand flat-footed for the first time in his life.

I knew that my sister and my niece had walked on their toes when they were babies, and they had learned to walk normally as adults. I also knew that if Quinn didn't learn to walk flat-footed, it would lead to problems with his mobility for the rest of his life. That scenario was unacceptable to me, and it scared me. After six months of wearing a brace and daily physical therapy, Quinn was walking normally. He didn't require physical therapy or a brace any longer, and I was happy about his progress.

However, Tori was concerned about Quinn's language. She worried that Quinn was having trouble hearing. We were off again to see another specialist. Quinn was seen by an audiologist, and it was determined that he had very poor hearing. An ear, nose, and throat specialist diagnosed Quinn with chronic middle ear fluid. So Quinn had tubes put in his ears and had his adenoids removed. We desperately hoped his hearing loss was responsible for his language delay. Somewhere in the back of my mind, the term *cerebral palsy* came creeping back in. I had almost ruled it out, because Quinn was walking so well.

We took Quinn to Tori's department at the university for a speech and language evaluation. Her department ran a master's-level clinical school for communication disorders. Quinn qualified for biweekly speech and language therapy. His progress was slow at first. As the weeks passed, I realized the gravity of the situation and started thinking about the future. Quinn could need lifelong support. I was thinking about opening my own business, so I could employ Quinn when he finished school. Quinn might need to be trained in a vocational skill, and we might need to help him support himself as an adult.

One of my greatest concerns as a father is how the other students in school will treat Quinn. I worry about Quinn being accepted socially. It's important that he fit in both at school and in the neighborhood. I want him to have a support system of family and friends that will allow him to be happy. Quinn came into our lives when we were older, so I worry about what he will do when we are gone. A lot of things, both big and small, occur to you when you are dealing with a child with a disability. All I can do is work with Quinn each day and hope for progress.

When Quinn turned three, he was evaluated for early childhood special education services through our school district, and he qualified for a half-day program. Although he is speaking in sentences now and is able to express his wants, needs, and feelings, he still lacks in vocabulary and ease of conversation. After a year of half-day services, Quinn will be attending the full-day program as a four-year-old in the fall. We plan on keeping Quinn in preschool until he goes to kindergarten at six years old. He will be a little older than the other students, but he needs the extra year to develop more language skills. Quinn recently saw a doctor who told us that he also had a language delay as a child. The doctor said his parents were very concerned about him as a child, but he "grew out" of his difficulties. I can only hope this will happen for Quinn as well.

> ## ▶▶ Questions to Ponder
>
> ▶ Whose story is this?
>
> ▶ What is my background or previous experience with the issues presented in this case?
>
> ▶ What facts are presented?
>
> ▶ What opinions are presented?

Tori McCloud's Story

For nineteen years, I have been in the field of special education. I have an undergraduate degree, master's degree, and doctorate in special education. I have had the privilege of working with many different children with disabilities and their families, and I've taught both undergraduate and graduate courses in special education. But it wasn't until recently that I learned, firsthand, the impact of having a child with a disability on a family. I used to think I knew so much, and now I know I have so much to learn. Even though I now have more questions than answers, I know I am a better professor and educator than I was before Quinn came into my life.

When my older son Brenden was born, I worried about his development. I was concerned when he didn't walk until thirteen months. But he started talking at twelve months and by two could hold a conversation with people on a variety of topics. So, when Quinn walked late and only had about seventy words at two, people told me not to worry and not to compare my kids. They said Quinn was the second child, and they usually talk later and walk later. But in the back of my head, I knew Quinn's development was different. This is when I began my search.

I started with a pediatric neurologist and orthopedic specialist. I knew it was unusual for Quinn to be unable to flatten his feet. That's why Scot and I first felt that Quinn might have a disability. The neurologist reported that Quinn didn't appear to have anything more than "congenital toe walking," but the orthopedic specialist said that Quinn appeared to have a mild form of monoplegia cerebral palsy. After hearing the term *cerebral palsy,* I knew that if this were the case, Quinn might also have other difficulties. I also knew Quinn's language was not where I expected it to be. But he was so young that no one seemed to think it was unusual. I took him to an audiologist because he didn't seem to respond to noise consistently. We found out he had chronic middle ear fluid and probably hadn't heard well for at least a year. Although he didn't have any symptoms of an ear infection, the fluid was affecting his hearing. At two and a half, Quinn had tubes placed in his ears, and his language began to improve. But the progress over the past year and a half has been slow, and every day I worry about his development. He has had physical therapy and speech and language therapy, and he now attends an early childhood special education program. I wish I could spend more time working with Quinn, but I have to leave that up to Scot who has more time. At least I get to read with Quinn every night. We work on basic concepts, "WH" questions, phonological awareness, and letter/number recognition.

My training in special education is both a blessing and a curse. I am trained to identify and remediate disabilities, but I frequently read too much into Quinn's behaviors. I often feel like I can't read my own son. I can pinpoint other children's difficulties and help their parents find answers and help, but I can't do that for my own child. As a special education professional, I find myself compelled to label my child. I want a diagnosis that will allow me to choose the correct remediation and help me plan for Quinn's education and quality of life. However, my child (like all children with disabilities) didn't come in a nice little category box. He is simply Quinn.

He has a mild motor delay, both his receptive and expressive language skills are a year behind his peers, and he insists on consistency in his daily routine. On the other hand, he is social, plays well with other children, engages in pretend and imaginary play, and is learning letters and numbers. He is a sweetheart who runs to the door every day after work and says, "Mommy, I guess you all finish work. I need big hugs and kisses." He calls me on the phone at work to say, "You need come home now so I can carry you." I know he means that he wants me to hold him. To me, he is just my little boy with strengths and weaknesses. As we make our journey together, as a family, we may have to support Quinn as an adult, or we may not. Either way, we will watch him soar. I am determined to do the best for Quinn, which means continuing my search to identify his needs and have them met at home and at school. I am lucky to have Scot, who is willing to take steps to ensure Quinn's success in life. I am also committed to making sure all educators see the importance of assisting families in their support of their own children. In the end, I know having Quinn has made me a better professional and a better person.

Brenden McCloud's Story

Sometimes it's hard to understand what my little brother, Quinn, is saying. Other kids can pretty much do stuff like talk easier, and you can understand them more. Quinn doesn't understand me either sometimes. When he can't understand me, he doesn't know what to do. I try to explain what things mean to him. If he doesn't understand he will watch, or he will kind of throw a fit and whine. Sometimes he will hit me, but not really hard. I know that means he is discouraged.

   I think it's kind of weird that Quinn goes to a different school. Most kids his age go to a regular preschool, but Quinn goes to school with kids who have disabilities. Some can't talk, or understand, or walk. I think it's sad that they aren't like other children. I don't really feel sorry for Quinn, because he can get better, and some children can't. I think he will get better. If he doesn't get better, I will help him out when he is a grown-up, because he is my brother. He loves me, and I love him.

Case Study Framework Questions

1. What makes this a contemplation case?
2. How do emotions influence behaviors in the main characters?
3. How is the factual information consistent with current professional literature?
4. Are issues oversimplified? If so, how?
5. Are people stereotyped? If so, how?

6. Discuss teacher dispositions that could facilitate interaction (i.e., self-reflection, tolerance for others, collaboration, multiple perspectives, sound ethical judgment, motivation to work with students with a variety of needs, capacity for advocacy) or that could become a barrier to working with the student discussed in the case.

Thinking Critically About the Case

1. What type of support has Quinn received from health, community, and school agencies?
2. What other professions should be involved in this case?
3. Families go through stages of shock, guilt, anger, depression, blame, denial, and finally acceptance when a child is diagnosed with a disability. Which of these stages can you identify in each story?
4. How do you think Quinn's case might have been different if his parents were not knowledgeable about disabilities and special education services?
5. What impact could having a sibling with a disability have on a child?

Activity

Valdivieso, Ripley, and Ambler (1988) have identified the following concerns related to having a sibling with a disability:

- Guilt about not having a disability
- Embarrassment over the sibling's behavior or appearance
- Fear that he or she might develop the disability
- Anger or jealousy over the amount of attention the brother or sister with a disability receives
- Isolation or feeling that no one else has the same feelings or experiences about having a sibling with a disability
- Pressure to achieve in order to "make up for" a brother or sister's inabilities
- Responsibility for caregiving or being expected to care for the sibling with a disability in the parent's absence at school or in the community

Brainstorm a list of possible actions that parents and teachers can take to ensure that the sibling's feelings are validated and that they are supported at home and school.

CASE 2 "Skylar"

Type of Case: Exemplar

Age Level: Early Childhood

Characters

Skylar Kirkpatrick, two-year-eleven-month-old girl

Tara Kirkpatrick, Skylar's mother

Dan Kirkpatrick, Skylar's father

Diagnostic Report

History of Presenting Complaint

Skylar Kirkpatrick, a two-year-eleven-month-old girl, was referred to the Child and Family Bridges Program by her pediatrician, Dr. Julianna Huges-Garrett. Mrs. Kirkpatrick reported that she and her husband have trouble understanding Skylar's speech. Skylar lives with Mr. and Mrs. Kirkpatrick and her brother Lucas, who is five years old.

Mrs. Kirkpatrick reported good general health during her pregnancy and a typical childbirth. Skylar met developmental milestones for sitting, crawling, walking, and talking later than her peers of the same age. Mr. Kirkpatrick reported that Skylar had seen an endocrinologist and geneticist because Skylar's pediatrician was worried about large growth spurts. The pediatrician was particularly concerned about Skylar's head circumference, which was in the 98th percentile. The report from the endocrinologist and geneticist, which was just received, indicated that Skylar tested positive for Sotos syndrome. Sotos syndrome, also known as cerebral gigantism because of the distinctive head shape and size, is a rare genetic condition causing physical growth during the first years of life. The rapid physical development is often accompanied by delayed motor, cognitive, and social development. Muscle tone is low and speech is markedly impaired. Although children with Sotos syndrome are often taller and heavier and have larger heads than their peers in early childhood, in late childhood the gap between their physical development and that of their peers begins to close.

Social and Emotional Status

Skylar Kirkpatrick lives with her parents and her older brother. English is the primary language spoken in the home. Skylar is described as being happy, energetic, and sometimes clingy. She exhibits acting-out behaviors when she is frustrated about her inability to communicate or be understood. When such behaviors occur, her parents typically use redirection or timeout. Mrs. Kirkpatrick reports that Skylar responds well to praise. Skylar's parents feel her language interferes with her level of independence, because she has difficulty communicating with others.

During the evaluation, Skylar appeared timid. Although she had difficulty separating from her parents, she did not exhibit any acting-out behaviors.

Assessments

Skylar was given selected subtests on the *Wechsler Intelligence Scale for Children-III* (Wechsler, 1991) to assess her cognitive functioning. Although rapport was easily established, when she went with the examiner she had some difficulty separating from her mother. Her overall composite score fell within the range of slightly below average (79). Her verbal reasoning score was the lowest. Short-term memory (estimate) fell within the average range. Although she was difficult to understand, Skylar appeared to have an emerging vocabulary and a strong short-term memory.

The *Battelle Developmental Inventory* (Newborg et al., 2004) was administered to assess Skylar's developmental status across several areas. Both Mr. and Mrs. Kirkpatrick were present and served as the informants for the interview section of the assessment. Skylar was shy and timid during the assessment but was not difficult to engage in the assessment activities. She cooperated fully throughout the session. The following is a summary of the assessment scores. Skylar scored within the low-average range in the areas of personal-social development and receptive communication. She showed a mild delay in the areas of fine motor development, gross motor development, adaptive behavior development, and cognitive development. In the area of motor development, Skylar was unable to walk upstairs alternating feet, walk backward, walk heel to toe, and jump up. She showed a moderate delay in the area of expressive communication. In summary, Skylar is a shy, yet friendly, toddler who is experiencing some difficulty within developmental areas such as motor development and cognitive development. She is having particular difficulty in the area of expressive communication.

The *Test of Oral Structures and Functions* (Vitali, 1986) was administered to Skylar to evaluate oral movements. Skylar had difficulty with blowing, puckering her lips, touching her nose with the tip of her tongue, biting her lower lip, whistling, clicking her tongue, chattering her teeth, touching her chin with the tip of her tongue, and wiggling her tongue from side to side. This is not uncommon for children with Sotos syndrome because of its associated hypotonia. Hypotonia causes poor facial muscle tone, which results in prolonged drooling and mouth breathing as well as difficulties with the tongue movement needed for speech. Skylar was able to perform the tasks of sticking out her tongue, showing her teeth, clearing her throat, coughing, and puffing out her cheeks.

The Assessment of Phonological Processing-Revised was administered to assess Skylar's phonological or sound-processing abilities. The results of this test indicate that Skylar has a profound phonological processing disorder. She consistently omits consonants in words that begin with consonant clusters. For instance, she says "gee" for "green" and "sop" for "stop." She also omits consonants at the end of words, saying "boo" for "book." Skylar's consonant phonetic repertoire includes the sounds /p/, /b/, /m/, /t/, /d/, /n/, /h/, /f/, /v/, /k/, /s/, and /g/.

▶▶ Questions to Ponder

▶ Whose story is this?

▶ What is my background or previous experience with the issues presented in this case?

▶ What facts are presented?

▶ What opinions are presented?

Summary

Skylar is an active and happy little girl who lives at home with her parents and brother. She was referred for assessment because of difficulty with intelligible speech. Results of the assessment indicate that Skylar has a mild delay in motor skills, both gross and fine, and a mild cognitive delay. She presents with a profound phonological disorder that is characterized by the use of deviant phonological processing, which makes her speech unintelligible to the average listener. Deficiencies in receptive language were not present at this time. Skylar qualifies for developmental therapy. She needs speech/language therapy and physical therapy to address her areas of delay. Skylar would benefit from attending the developmental play group offered by the Child and Family Bridges Program twice a week for 60 minutes. She would also benefit from in-home physical therapy and speech/language therapy two times per month for 60 minutes through the Child and Family Bridges Program.

Treatment Plan

Long Term Goal 1: Skylar will increase her intelligibility through remediation of phonological processes.

Objectives	Baseline Percentage	Current Percentage
Skylar will produce two-syllable words after a verbal model from the clinician with 90% accuracy.	85	
When shown a picture of an object and asked to name the object, Skylar will produce two-syllable words without a verbal model from the clinician with 90% accuracy.	80	
When shown a picture of an object and asked to name the object, Skylar will produce final consonants in a CVC (consonant-vowel-consonant) and VC (vowel-consonant) word after a verbal model with 90% accuracy (words such as *cat* and *up*).	33	
When shown a picture of an object and asked to name the object, Skylar will produce final consonants in a CVC (consonant-vowel-consonant) and VC (vowel-consonant) word without a verbal model with 90% accuracy (words such as *cat* and *up*).	0	

Long Term Goal 2: Skylar will increase oral motor strength through practice with oral motor exercises.

Objectives	Baseline Percentage	Current Percentage
Given a verbal prompt and modeling, Skylar will be able to make 7 of the 9 mouth movements for: blowing, puckering of lips, touching her nose with the tip of her tongue, biting her lower lip, whistling, clicking her tongue, chattering her teeth, touching her chin with the tip of her tongue, and wiggling her tongue from side to side.	0	

Case Study Framework Questions

1. What makes this an exemplar case?
2. How do emotions influence behaviors in the main characters?
3. How is the factual information consistent with current professional literature?
4. Are issues oversimplified? If so, how?
5. Are people stereotyped? If so, how?
6. Discuss teacher dispositions that could facilitate interaction (e.g., self-reflection, tolerance for others, collaboration, multiple perspectives, sound ethical judgment, motivation to work with students with a variety of needs, capacity for advocacy) or that could become a barrier to working with the student discussed in the case.

Thinking Critically About the Case

1. What is Sotos syndrome?
2. What assessments were used to determine Skylar's strengths and weaknesses?
3. What are Skylar's strengths and weaknesses as determined by the testing?
4. In what standard deviation would Skylar fall for cognitive development, using the bell curve with a mean of 100 and a standard deviation of 15, which is used on the *Wechsler Intelligence Scale for Children-III*?

Activity

The long-term goal is that Skylar will improve her gross motor skills by participating in physical therapy. Write an objective for the skills she was unable to perform as reported in the *Battelle Developmental Inventory*. Use the following framework (baseline 0%):

Given . . ., *or* When presented with . . .,
Skylar will be able to . . .
with _____% accuracy or on _____ of _____ trials.

REFERENCES

Newborg, J., Stock, J. R., Wnek, L., Guidubaldi, J., & Svinicki, J. (2004). *Battelle Developmental Inventory* (2nd ed.). Itasca, IL: Riverside.

Valdivieso, C., Ripley, S., & Ambler, L. (1988). Children with disabilities: Understanding sibling issues. *NICHCY News Digest,* Number 11. Washington, DC: Interstate Research Associates.

Vitali, G. (1986). *The Test of Oral Structures and Functions.* East Aurora, NY: Slosson Educational Publications, Inc.

Wechsler, D. (1991). *Wechsler Intelligence Scale for Children–III* (3rd ed.). San Antonio, TX: Psychological Corporation.

RESOURCES FOR FURTHER INVESTIGATION

Print

Brice, A., & Roseberry-MeKibbin, C. (2001). Choice of languages in instruction: One language or two? *Teaching Exceptional Children, 33*(4), 10–16.

Hancock, T. B., Kaiser, A. P., & Delaney, E. M. (2002). Teaching parents of preschoolers at risk. *Topics in Early Childhood Special Education, 22*(4), 191–213.

Harbin, G. L., Bruder, M. B., Adams, C., Mazzarella, C., Whitbread, K., Gabbard, G., & Staff, I. (2004). Early head start: Identifying and serving children with disabilities. *Topics in Early Childhood Special Education, 24*(2), 89–98.

Honig, A. (2001). Language flowering, language empowering: 20 ways parents and teachers can assist young children. *Montessori Life, 13*(4), 31–34.

Hull, K., Goldhaber, J., & Capone, A. (2002). *Opening doors: An introduction to inclusive early childhood education.* Boston: Houghton Mifflin.

Salend, S., & Salinas, A. (2003). Language differences or learning difficulties. *Teaching Exceptional Children, 35*(4), 36–43.

Web

Division for Early Childhood
http://www.dec-sped.org/index.html

Sotos Syndrome Support Association
http://www.well.com/user/sssa

Chapter 3

Cases Involving Students Who Are Gifted and Talented

CASE 1 "Carolyn"

Type of Case: **Exemplar**

Age Level: **Elementary School**

Characters

Carolyn McGlasson, fourth-grade student

Anna Grayton, fourth-grade teacher

Adam Kaufman, sixth-grade teacher

Gina Sego, third-grade teacher

Susan Wilson, first-grade teacher

Christy Bud, school psychologist

Carolyn leaned back in her chair and began to whisper to Ahmed, the child sitting next to her. Ahmed laughed aloud. Carolyn then leaned over to Jamie, the child in front of her, and told the same joke, laughing as she whispered. Jamie also began to laugh. The rest of the class was quiet and working on a math worksheet. Mrs. Grayton, Carolyn's teacher, got up from her desk and said, "Carolyn, have you completed your work?" Carolyn nodded yes. "Then you will need to move your chair into the hallway again," Mrs. Grayton stated. Carolyn quietly stood up and moved her desk to the hallway. While sitting in the hallway for the next 20 minutes, Carolyn looked out the window, hummed, and daydreamed. At the end of math class, she moved her desk back into the classroom. During English class that afternoon, the class was asked to finish a worksheet on nouns. After 5 minutes, Carolyn completed the worksheet and again began to talk to the children around her as they worked. Mrs. Grayton again moved Carolyn to the hallway.

During the first month of school, Carolyn seemed to spend as much time in the hallway as in class. After one occasion, Mrs. Grayton contacted Carolyn's mother by telephone. She stated, "I just don't know what is wrong with Carolyn. She does well on her written work, but she just cannot stop bothering other students. I have talked to her over and over again and she doesn't respond. The only thing I can do is to send her to the hallway so that she doesn't disturb other children. I'm beginning to wonder if other issues, perhaps emotional, are affecting her."

Carolyn's mother was at a loss to explain what was happening. Carolyn had always been a bright, verbal child. She learned to read before attending kindergarten and was completing complex math problems as a preschooler. In fact, when Carolyn was only two years old, she was counting objects using one-to-one correspondence. In addition, Carolyn was always very active and impulsive, which sometimes got her into trouble.

> ▶▶ **Questions to Ponder**
>
> ▶ Whose story is this?
>
> ▶ What is my background or previous experience with the issues presented in this case?
>
> ▶ What facts are presented?
>
> ▶ What opinions are presented?

After the first month of school, Mrs. Grayton did not know how to proceed in helping Carolyn with her behavior. She decided to take her concerns to the building Teacher Assistance Team for ideas. This was a team composed of four teachers and the school psychologist whose purpose was to assist teachers in developing strategies to help children. The team identified a child's needs, gathered data, helped develop strategies for meeting those needs, assisted in interventions, and monitored the child's progress. Although Mrs. Grayton was familiar with the team, she had never taken a case to the team and felt somewhat insecure about asking for help. However, Carolyn really needed intervention, and Mrs. Grayton didn't know how to help. After speaking with the chairperson of the team, Mrs. Grayton was given a one-page form, Consultation Team Request, which she completed and returned.

The teacher assistance team sent Mrs. Grayton a note inviting her to a meeting to discuss Carolyn after school the following Thursday. At the meeting, the following persons were present: Mr. Kaufman, sixth-grade teacher; Ms. Sego, third-grade teacher; Ms. Wilson, first-grade teacher; and Ms. Bud, school psychologist. Mr. Kaufman began the meeting by saying, "Anna, we received your request for assistance in working with Carolyn McGlasson and we will begin the discussion today. We are not here to tell you what to do, but to help define your concerns, gather information, generate possible interventions, assist you in carrying out the interventions, and evaluate the interventions." Anna began by telling the team about Carolyn and her concerns about Carolyn's behavior. She said

---

CONSULTATION TEAM REQUEST

Student Name: Carolyn McGlasson   **Date of Birth:** Nov. 11, 1995

Teacher Name: Anna Grayton   **Grade:** 4

Date of Request: October 15, 2004

1. **Reason for referral.** Carolyn spends most of her time in the hallway because she disturbs the class and misbehaves. When students are working independently, Carolyn finishes her work quickly and then bothers other children to the point that they cannot complete the work. She tells jokes, laughs, talks out loud, and fidgets with objects in her desk. When I move her to the hallway, she doesn't seem to mind. Even during class discussions, Carolyn often talks out impulsively, without raising her hand.

2. **Describe the interventions you have tried to resolve the problem.** I talked to Carolyn and told her the classroom rules. I talked with Carolyn's mother, who doesn't know why she does this. I also talked with Carolyn's teacher from last year, who said that she had the same problems. Moving her into the hallway is the only action that works.

3. **Does this child receive any special services? If so, describe the services.** No special services.

4. **Does this child have any medical, social, or emotional problems that might influence progress in the classroom?** I wonder if emotional problems might be a contributing factor. Socially, Carolyn seems immature and impulsive. She often blurts out in class and says unkind things to other children. Other children don't like to play with her. There are no medical problems.

5. **What concerns would you like addressed by the team?** How can I help Carolyn stop disturbing others in class? Why does she misbehave in class?

Please bring work samples or documentation that reflects this child's difficulty.

---

that Carolyn often spent considerable time in the hallway for misbehavior. When asked about Carolyn's academic skills, Anna stated that Carolyn was very bright and almost always completed her work. The team reviewed Carolyn's permanent school record and noted that she had exceeded state standards on the State Achievement Test given last year. On a standardized group intelligence test given in third grade, Carolyn performed at the 96th percentile when compared to other children her age. Anna acknowledged that Carolyn was generally a good student but that her behavior interfered with her progress. One team member wondered aloud if Carolyn might be bored with the work and if it might be too easy for her. Anna said that she had not really considered this, but that it certainly was possible. The team decided to have a member observe Carolyn in class and then discuss interventions the next week. After the observation, the team met again. After a lengthy discussion of data gathered during the observation (baseline data), the team drafted a written plan, and Anna agreed to try the interventions for six weeks. During the intervention, Anna agreed to gather data about the target behavior. At the end of that time, Anna would report back to the team.

On December 15, the team met after school to review Carolyn's progress and the success of the intervention. Mrs. Grayton said, "I just can't believe the difference this has made for Carolyn. She has made tremendous progress! She rarely disturbs other children now. She is reading very sophisticated books and loves receiving extra credit. In fact, she reads a

---

CONSULTATION TEAM INTERVENTION PLAN

Student Name: Carolyn McGlasson   **Date of Birth:** Nov. 11, 1995

Teacher Name: Anna Grayton   **Grade:** 4

Date of Consultation Meeting: November 1, 2004

Target Behaviors/Deficit(s): Carolyn will not disturb other children (e.g., talk out loud, talk to other children) during independent work time.

Intervention (Strategies, Techniques, Adaptations): Mrs. Grayton will meet with Carolyn during recess to talk with her about a behavior contract. The contract will state that Carolyn can choose a book of interest (her favorite activity) to read any time she completes her assigned work. When Carolyn completes her work, she should raise her hand and Mrs. Grayton will collect the work. Carolyn can then read quietly until the next subject begins. After Carolyn completes a book, she can write a short summary of it for extra credit and go to the library to choose another book at the end of the day.

Data to Be Gathered: Mrs. Grayton will ask Carolyn to sign the contract. She will then keep a daily chart indicating the presence or absence of the target behavior. She will write the data on a graph and bring the graph to the next team meeting.

Scheduled Review Date: December 15

Participants: Mrs. Grayton, Mr. Kaufman, Ms. Sego, Ms. Wilson, Ms. Bud

book every week or so. She also seems more engaged in class and calmer. I have written her mother a note telling her about her improvement." Mrs. Grayton shared the graph that she had been keeping on the target behavior. At the beginning of the intervention, Carolyn rarely achieved the target behavior, and now she achieved it all of the time. The team considered the case a success, and Carolyn was never referred again.

Case Study Framework Questions

1. What makes this an exemplar case?
2. How do emotions influence behaviors in the main characters?
3. How is the factual information consistent with current professional literature?
4. Are issues oversimplified? If so, how?
5. Are people stereotyped? If so, how?
6. Discuss teacher dispositions that could facilitate interaction (e.g., self-reflection, tolerance for others, collaboration, multiple perspectives, sound ethical judgment, motivation to work with students with a variety of needs, capacity for advocacy) or that could become a barrier to working with the student discussed in the case.

Thinking Critically About the Case

1. Do you think Carolyn was gifted? Why or why not?
2. Describe the process used to develop interventions for Carolyn.
3. What collaboration strategies did the general and special educators use?
4. What classroom strategies were used to increase Carolyn's success in the general education classroom?
5. Describe Carolyn's response to the interventions.
6. What other professionals should be involved, and what should they be doing?

Activity

Locate a copy of the Individuals with Disabilities Education Improvement Act (IDEA). Review the section concerning referral and evaluation for special education services. Does IDEA address prereferral intervention systems? If so, how are they addressed? If not, do you think the prereferral intervention system should be included? Why?

CASE 2 "Chancellor"

Type of Case: Contemplation

Age Level: Elementary School

Characters

Chancellor Nicholson, fifth-grade student

Eva Nicholson, Chancellor's mother

Bill Browning, fifth-grade teacher

Sandra Wilson, principal

Chancellor's day began in the same way that most days began. He ate a big breakfast, and then his mother quickly rushed him and his older brother out of the house at precisely 8:00 A.M. His mother always insisted that both boys never be late to school. Chancellor knew he had to take some kind of test today to see who would be eligible for the school "Talents" or gifted program. He wanted to be included, but he didn't say anything to his mother or friends about his wishes. His mother received a typed letter from the teacher indicating that all children would take an intelligence test to determine inclusion in the "Talents" program. Knowing that Chancellor was nervous about tests, his mother said not to worry about how he did, just to do his best work. Chancellor's mother was a school psychologist for a neighboring school district. She felt that children were given too many tests in school and that many were not necessary. She wondered about why an entire class must take an intelligence test.

Chancellor was a bright, curious child in school and home. Since he began school, he displayed unusual interests and abilities for his age level. He learned very quickly and was able to reason and problem-solve at a high level. His favorite subject was math, and he was placed in the advanced math class. Even so, he rarely had homework because he usually completed it at school. Reading and writing were less favored, but he always earned above-average grades in his subjects. The children at school and in the neighborhood liked and admired Chancellor, and he was viewed as a leader, even with older children. His interests included rock climbing, scuba diving, and nuclear power.

Chancellor had an unusual ability to work with people, adults, and children. He seemed to sense how people felt and responded in a very mature manner for his age.

Chancellor was normally a very quiet, sensitive, and conscientious student in school. On the day of the test, he put his books in his locker, listened to the daily announcements, and listened as his teacher, Mr. Browning, told students the daily schedule. In the morning, students would take the test, then go to lunch and recess. After lunch, they would have social studies, science, and physical education. Chancellor felt somewhat uptight about tests and especially about this test, because it seemed important.

> ▶▶ **Questions to Ponder**
>
> ▶ Whose story is this?
>
> ▶ What is my background or previous experience with the issues presented in this case?
>
> ▶ What facts are presented?
>
> ▶ What opinions are presented?

At 9:00 A.M., Mr. Browning handed out test booklets, answer sheets, and pencils. After a short introduction, the first subtest, reading, began. Chancellor put forth his best effort, but he thought to himself that the test seemed very difficult. During the second subtest, writing, the test seemed even more difficult, and Chancellor was becoming upset. This frustrating feeling continued throughout two more subtests. The last subtest was math, and Mr. Browning handed out scratch paper before the test began. As he walked around the room, Mr. Browning noticed that some students had different test booklets than others. As he looked more closely, he realized that about half of the class of twenty-five students had been taking the seventh-grade version of the test! Mr. Browning told the class that a mistake had been made and that the class would finish the morning taking the fifth-grade math test. After lunch, the sixteen students who had taken the seventh-grade test would come back and take the fifth-grade version of the test. Chancellor was in the group who had taken the seventh-grade test, and he was tearful as he left the room. After lunch, the students came back to take the fifth-grade test.

When Chancellor came home that afternoon, he told his mother that he had a headache. He also seemed upset and was tearful. After talking about his day, he burst out with what had happened. His mother said not to worry about the test, but she quietly decided that she would visit the teacher and the principal the next day.

That evening, Mrs. Nicholson read the student handbook section on the criteria for the "Talents" program. The handbook said that students would be included in the pullout program based on three factors: intelligence test score (95th percentile or above), achievement test scores (one area or more in the 95th percentile or above), and teacher recommendation. All three factors had to be met for inclusion in the program. The program consisted of two 30-minute enrichment sessions per week with a teacher of the gifted. Chancellor's mother knew that he had special talents, but she wasn't interested in his inclusion in the program. Instead, she was concerned about the purpose of the test and the test conditions, because Chancellor was very upset.

The next morning, after Chancellor left for school, Mrs. Nicholson walked into the school office and asked if she could make an appointment with the school principal, Mrs. Wilson. Mrs. Wilson came out of her office and offered to meet with Mrs. Nicholson at that time. After they were seated at a round table in Mrs. Wilson's office, the conference began.

Mrs. Nicholson began by saying, "Mrs. Wilson, I understand that the fifth-grade class took an intelligence test yesterday."

Mrs. Wilson responded, "Yes, they took the test to help identify students for the 'Talents' program."

Mrs. Nicholson continued, "I am concerned about the testing conditions and the effect on Chancellor's score. I understand that about half of the class was given several subtests from the seventh-grade version of the test. Then, after the error was discovered, students finished the morning taking the fifth-grade test. After lunch, the students who took the seventh-grade version had to take the test again at the fifth-grade level. I am concerned about the stress that Chancellor felt taking the seventh-grade test and its effect on his performance on the fifth-grade test. I am also concerned that the test publisher probably didn't intend for the test to be given in this manner. In fact, I question the reliability, and therefore validity, of the scores for those children."

Mrs. Wilson said, "Why?"

Mrs. Nicholson said, "As you know, to be a valid assessment of a child's abilities, tests must produce consistent results, or be reliable. The test has to be given under standard conditions, and I don't think this test was given under standard conditions. Giving the wrong test for most of the morning has to influence the child's results. Therefore, if Chancellor were given the test again, I feel certain that he would have different results. This also makes the results invalid."

Mrs. Wilson answered, "I know about the mistake, and it wasn't the teacher's fault. Apparently, the test booklets were delivered from another school, where they were not properly placed in the grade-level boxes. The teacher assumed that he was handing out the fifth-grade test, but I think the mistake was corrected after the first subtest."

"That isn't my understanding," Mrs. Nicholson said. "Chancellor said the children took four subtests before the mistake was corrected. Chancellor was very upset and frustrated when he came home. I know his feelings of frustration affected his performance on the test."

Mrs. Wilson said defensively, "I really wasn't aware that students took four seventh-grade subtests. However, at least the mistake was corrected and students took the fifth-grade test. Anyway, this test just confirms how students performed on the group achievement test. It doesn't really mean anything."

Mrs. Nicholson stated, "I don't understand how an intelligence test could confirm how students perform on a group achievement test. I really hope important decisions will not be based on this test. I don't think the test could be reliable or valid given the manner in which it was given."

Mrs. Wilson said, "Well, if the test scores were high for the group, do you think they would be valid?"

Mrs. Nicholson said, "No, I don't. I think it might be a good idea for you to contact the test company to see if these scores should be used."

Mrs. Wilson ended by saying, "Of course we'll check into this, Mrs. Nicholson. Thank you for coming in today."

Mrs. Nicholson was less than satisfied, but decided to let the matter go. It didn't really matter if Chancellor was included in the "Talents" program. It was more important to her that he was learning and his teacher was challenging him. In the end, Chancellor was not invited to join the program. Mrs. Nicholson felt some relief because she didn't want him to be taken out of class for the enrichment program.

Case Study Framework Questions

1.   What makes this a contemplation case?
2.   How do emotions influence behaviors in the main characters?
3.   How is the factual information consistent with current professional literature?
4.   Are issues oversimplified? If so, how?
5.   Are people stereotyped? If so, how?
6.   Discuss teacher dispositions that could facilitate interaction (i.e., self-reflection, tolerance for others, collaboration, multiple perspectives, sound ethical judgment, motivation to work with students with a variety of needs, capacity for advocacy) or that could become a barrier to working with the student discussed in the case.

Thinking Critically About the Case

1.   Upon what basis are children generally identified for gifted programs?
2.   How did the criteria used in Chancellor's school compare with that basis?
3.   Test "reliability" refers to consistency. If a test is administered two times to the same child, the results will be similar. However, the test must be administered in the same manner each time (e.g., same instructions, same general testing conditions). How is test reliability of the intelligence test important in this case?
4.   Validity is whether or not the test assesses what it purports to measure. A test cannot be valid if it is unreliable. How is validity of the intelligence test important in this case?
5.   What other professionals should be involved, and what should they be doing?

Activity

You are Chancellor's classroom teacher. Write a short note to the "Talents" teacher explaining why you think Chancellor belongs in the program. Include your observations of him in class, his learning characteristics, why the intelligence test might not be a reliable and valid assessment of his abilities, and how you think the program would enhance his education.

RESOURCES FOR FURTHER INVESTIGATION

Print

Clark, B. (2002). *Growing up gifted: Developing the potential of children at home and school* (6th ed.). Upper Saddle River, NJ: Merrill/Prentice-Hall.

Cline, S., & Hegeman, K. (2001). Gifted children with disabilities. *Gifted Child Today, 24*(3), 16–24.

Rotigel, J. (2003). Understanding the young gifted child: Guidelines for parents, families, and educators. *Early Childhood Education Journal, 30*(4), 209–214.

Winebrenner, S. (2000). Gifted students need an education, too. *Educational Leadership, 58*(1), 52–56.

Web

The Association for the Gifted (TAG), Council for Exceptional Children
http://www.cectag.org

Chapter 4

Cases Involving Students with Mental Impairment and Developmental Disabilities

CASE 1 "Sydney"

Type of Case: **Contemplation**

Age Level: **High School**

Characters

>   *Sydney Galinski,* ninth-grade girl
>
>   *Melinda Phelps,* ninth-grade special education teacher
>
>   *Allen Sears,* ninth-grade coach

Mr. Sears's Side

I can't believe Melinda Phelps! It's like she thinks I might have some kind of "intentions" toward Sydney. She is really overreacting to a simple mistake made by one of her students. She doesn't realize the history behind the situation.

Madison is a small town and a small community. The elementary, middle school, and high school are all in two buildings in the same block. I grew up here. Melinda sure didn't. I've known the Galinski family all my life. In fact, Sydney's aunt and my mom were best friends all through school. Which means I've known Sydney since she was born. I remember her parents taking her to town events in a baby stroller when I was in eighth grade.

Everyone in town felt so sorry for them. Sydney has Down syndrome and has had so many health problems. She had four heart surgeries before she was three years old. When she was a baby, she had problems with spitting up. She was really small, because she had so much difficulty keeping food down. She still has stomach problems, even though she is not small for her age anymore. She also has trouble with loose joints, so her hips and shoulders dislocate easily. I can remember at least four dislocations. We all love Sydney. Sure, she could have her temper tantrums and misbehaviors, like any kid, but basically she has always been a sweet kid.

When she was in elementary school, she would refuse to come in from recess. The teacher would stand at the door and yell, "Sydney, Sydney, Sydney," and she would lie in the grass and pretend not to hear.

Finally, the teacher decided to have snack time right after recess, and that did the trick. Sydney would always do anything for chocolate. Now that she is getting older, she is getting overweight. It's also harder for her to exercise because her muscle tone is low. Being from the field of kinesiology and health, that worries me.

Anyway, the point is that I know Sydney and her family. I also know that Sydney has a little crush on me, and she has for years. It's cute. I mean, she really is more like a five-year-old than a sixteen-year-old. So, what's the harm? Sydney comes to my office every morning before school to talk. I think it makes her feel special that I look forward to seeing her. She also tries to come to as many basketball games as she can because I'm the coach. She wears her spirit shirt and shakes her pompoms, and I wave to her. It's not my idea to give her a hug every time I see her in the hall. She's the one who always wants to hug me. I'm not going to hurt her feelings by telling her no. I think that would be wrong. I did tell her that she was too old to hold hands with her teachers. She looked so hurt. I'm not going to stop being her friend just because her new special education teacher wants me too. Melinda Phelps just moved to Madison, so she doesn't have the full story. I know that she's been teaching a lot longer than I have, but she doesn't know Sydney the way I do.

I have to admit I felt uncomfortable when Sydney showed me the new bra she had on, in the middle of the hall. When the other kids started laughing, she looked truly embarrassed and pulled her shirt down really fast. But Melinda is blowing this whole thing out of proportion. Sydney knew that was a mistake, and she will never do it again.

Now Melinda wants me to tell Sydney it's inappropriate to hug me and come see me every day before school. I think Melinda needs to loosen up and treat Sydney like the kid she really is!

▶▶ **Questions to Ponder**

▶ Whose story is this?

▶ What is my background or previous experience with the issues presented in this case?

▶ What facts are presented?

▶ What opinions are presented?

Mrs. Phelps's Side

Allen Sears seems to be a nice kid. He's only been teaching one year, but he seems to enjoy teaching. He has a great reputation with the students, and they all seem to worship him, especially the girls. He jokes around with the kids, and they eat it up. He still thinks that teachers can be friends also. That's a fallacy many new teachers make. New teachers are often afraid to discipline or correct student behavior because they "won't be liked anymore." I've heard the way the kids talk to Coach Sears in the hall. They call him "the man," and frankly, I think it's out of place. But he doesn't realize what he is doing with Sydney.

I just started working at Madison High School three years ago, teaching students with cognitive disabilities. Some have mild disabilities, and some have moderate disabilities. I have ninth-, tenth-, eleventh-, and twelfth-graders. This is my first year working with Sydney Galinski. She is a very nice student. However, her behavior is inappropriate with young men. I noticed that she started stopping by Allen Sears's office every day before school at the beginning of the school year. The para-educator who picks the kids up from the bus and walks or wheels them to my class makes a detour so Sydney can visit with Coach Sears. Sometimes the students will be late getting to class because Sydney has to say "hi." Every time she sees Allen, she has to give him this big hug, and, earlier in the year, she would hold his hand as she talked.

I take the students out into the community to develop functional life skills. We go to the Laundromat to wash clothes, go bowling once a week, visit job sites to work on transition skills, go shopping, to the bank, etc. Recently, Sydney has started hugging every young man she sees, even if she doesn't know him. And everyone seems to accept this. I read in Sydney's records that she was caught shoplifting last year, but nothing was done about it because "Sydney didn't understand what she was doing." Also, the storeowner didn't want to upset her. Just because she has a cognitive delay doesn't mean that she doesn't understand. People are underestimating her intelligence.

I think part of the problem stems from the fact that Sydney has had some significant health issues. I believe her parents were told she was unlikely to survive the heart surgeries she had as a baby. Because of that, she has been very overprotected and even babied. At the beginning of the year, her parents didn't want me to work on functional math with Sydney because she doesn't like it and they want her to like school and to like her teachers. I don't teach skills based on what the students like to do. I try to incorporate their interests into the lessons. However, just because you don't like math doesn't mean you don't have to do math!

Back to the issue with Allen Sears. I think he doesn't understand the depth of the issue. It's not that Sydney hugs him. It's that she is starting to hug every young man she meets. Her cognitive ability may be at a four- to five-year-old level, but physically she is a young woman. She is developing sexually, and she is having sexual urges. I've had to discuss the inappropriateness of touching yourself at school with her once this year. If I told Allen Sears that, he would probably be so embarrassed that he'd never speak to me again. But Sydney's just a normal sixteen-year-old girl interested in boys. She doesn't have the cognitive skills to understand her urges and how to act on them appropriately. So, we have to teach her! If someone doesn't teach her, she is going to be at risk for sexual abuse. I read one statistic saying three out of every four young women with cognitive disabilities will be sexually abused at least once in their life. I just don't want Sydney to be one of those women.

She has to learn how to interact appropriately with men. I'm worried about her safety. I know her crush is harmless, and Allen isn't interested in Sydney. However, it still isn't proper social behavior. The fact that Sydney pulled up her shirt in the middle of the hall to show Allen her new bra was just the final straw. Now, I know I have to do something. This is getting out of hand. I talked to him, but he isn't listening. Why can't Sydney give him a "high five" instead of a hug? Why can't he be unavailable before school a couple of times a week? Why can't *he* talk to her about appropriate behavior? I've tried, but if he doesn't follow through, it's a waste of time. Which is more important, being Sydney's friend or teaching her a skill she can use in the future that will keep her safe? She needs to learn how to act as a sexually mature young woman, not a five-year-old girl.

Case Study Framework Questions

1. What makes this a contemplation case?
2. How do emotions influence behaviors in the main characters?
3. How is the factual information consistent with current professional literature?
4. Are issues oversimplified? If so, how?
5. Are people stereotyped? If so, how?

6. Discuss teacher dispositions that could facilitate interaction (i.e., self-reflection, tolerance for others, collaboration, multiple perspectives, sound ethical judgment, motivation to work with students with a variety of needs, capacity for advocacy) or that could become a barrier to working with the student discussed in the case.

Thinking Critically About the Case

1. What does Allen Sears want? What does Melinda Phelps want?
2. How is Allen's perception of Sydney different from Melinda's?
3. How would you teach Sydney about appropriate interactions with the opposite sex?
4. How can teachers maintain appropriate boundaries with students?

Activity

Research commercially produced sex education and social skills training materials for use with students with disabilities. Choose a product. List the materials, name the publisher, and briefly describe the intended audience, skills taught, and your evaluation of the product.

Case 2 "Miki"

Type of Case: **Exemplar**

Age Level: **Middle School**

Characters

Miki Luo, sixth-grade girl diagnosed with a mild cognitive disability

Zenia Luo, Miki's mother

Mary Paulovich, sixth-grade special education teacher

Amelia Taylor, assistive technology consultan

Miki Luo is a sixth-grade student on my caseload. After working with her for only 3 months, I have noticed she is having difficulty transitioning from the elementary to the middle school setting. Her difficulties in academic tasks, compounded by difficulties with organization, study skills, reading, note taking, and attention, are beginning to affect her grades in content area classes. Instructionally, Miki is working on a low fourth-grade level in most of her academic areas and is included in general education classes for math, science, and social studies. She is pulled out for special education classes in reading/language arts and for resource assistance with her work assigned in the general education classes. Although she understands the material in math, science, and social studies, she is making poor grades because she is unable to demonstrate her knowledge on assignments and tests. She is not turning in assignments and is making poor grades on tests. Therefore, I have decided to discuss Miki's case with Amelia Taylor, the assistive technology consultant for my school district. Amelia asked that I write a description of Miki and send it to her before the meeting. This would allow her to get an idea of Miki's strengths and weaknesses and the type of assistive technology that might help Miki. Here is the report I sent to Amelia:

```
Miki is a sixth-grade student at Hawthorn Middle School.
She has had a history of special needs beginning with
birth. She was premature at birth, weighing only 2 pounds.
In kindergarten she was diagnosed with a mild cognitive
delay. Her measured IQ score was 62. In addition to a
cognitive delay, Miki also has a mild motor delay. She
```

(continued)

received physical therapy in kindergarten through third
grade for fine motor skills. Her fine motor weaknesses make
the task of writing difficult. Miki is left-handed and has
an incorrect pencil grasp. She also tends to fatigue easily
when doing written work. She does better typing her written
work on a computer, but her keyboarding skills are very
slow. However, she does enjoy this task.

Miki is mainstreamed into the general education classes for
math, science, and social studies. Although she is working
below grade level, accommodations and adaptations made by
the general education teachers help her be successful in
these areas. Although math is Miki's strength, she is
making a C- in class because she fails to turn in assignments on time or forgets to study for tests. I have
suggested pulling Miki into special education class for
math, but Zenia Luo, Miki's mother, is against that idea.
She believes pulling Miki into special education is only
allowing her to maintain her poor work and study habits.
Miki's grades are also dropping in science and social
studies classes because of her inability to independently
read and her poor organization and study skills.

Miki is pulled into special education for reading and
language arts. Her instructional level for reading is
presently at the upper third-grade level. Miki's reading
level interferes with her ability to read her textbooks to
gain information. Miki's mother has been reading all of
Miki's work to her, but she feels Miki needs help with
reading that will make her an independent reader. She also
needs someone to read tests to her.

Additionally, Miki has attention problems. She is rarely on
task. Because of her cognitive delay, Miki's attention and
concentration skills are more like a fourth-grader than a
sixth-grader. Zenia Luo would like to see the teachers
address her attention problems in school. Miki wants to do
well in school and has a very positive attitude, but her
deficits are making her feel like a failure. She has
started to complain about school. She says she feels lost
in the larger middle school.

In summary, Miki's biggest difficulties at school include
(1) reading the content textbooks, like the science and
social studies books, (2) taking notes, (3) using organizational skills, (4) using study skills, and (5) being
attentive and remaining on task. We are looking for ways to
support her at school using assistive technology.

▶▶ **Questions to Ponder**

▶ Whose story is this?

▶ What is my background or previous experience with the issues presented in this case?

▶ What facts are presented?

▶ What opinions are presented?

Amelia Taylor met with Zenia Luo, Miki Luo, Mary Paulovich, and Starla Wright, the sixth-grade social studies teacher, to discuss assistive technology options for Miki. Amelia defined assistive technology as any item, piece of equipment, or product system, whether acquired commercially or off the shelf, modified, or customized, that is used to increase, maintain, or improve the functional capabilities of children with disabilities. She also described the seven functional areas for which assistive technology is typically used: (1) existence/daily living; (2) communication; (3) body support, protection, and positioning; (4) travel and mobility; (5) environmental interaction; (6) education and transition; and (7) sports, fitness, and recreation. We all agreed that Miki could use assistive technology primarily in the area of education. Amelia explained how important it was to include Miki in the choice of assistive technology. After all, Miki is going to be the person using the device, and if she feels conspicuous then she probably won't use the device. Amelia then presented the group with a menu or list of options for each area in which Miki might be able to use assistive technology.

Assistive Technology Area	Device	Description
Reading content text	☐ Textbooks on tape ☐ Content videos in each subject ☐ Reading pen ☐ PowerPoint presentations in class ☐ Content websites with a screen reader	Reading pens scan text and pronounce words. They will also give the definition of words. These pens help students read independently when they need help with only specific vocabulary or particular words.

Assistive Technology Area	Device	Description
Note taking	☐ Speech-to-text software ☐ Copy of another student's notes ☐ Hand-held tape recorder ☐ A portable keyboard or note taker such as Alpha Smarts ☐ Prewritten outlines given by teacher ☐ Pencil grips or weighted pencils ☐ A slant board ☐ Modified keyboards ☐ Keyboarding instruction and software	Speech-to-text software would allow Miki to listen to another student's notes on a tape recorder and then talk into the computer. The computer would then transform the spoken word into text. This would allow Miki to identify relevant information from lectures and limit notes to include only important details. A slant board, pencil grip, and/or weighted pencil could help Miki with her fatigue when doing handwriting. Miki might also want to type her notes using a modified keyboard. The keyboard might have larger or smaller keys or be shaped differently to allow better positioning
Organizational skills	☐ Agenda book with assignment calendar ☐ Assignment checklist ☐ Picture schedule ☐ Hand-held organizer	An agenda book or notebook with folders for each class would help Miki organize each class. The folders could be color-coded. A checklist for "to do" things and pending assignments on the front of each folder would allow Miki and her parents to see what she needed to do and turn in. The completed work would be placed in the folder and turned in the next day. Her teachers and parents might check her folder daily to help

Assistive Technology Area	Device	Description
		Miki organize herself. A hand-held organizer could contain Miki's calendar, notes, and checklists and have an alarm to remind her to do things.
Study skills	☐ Tape-recorded directions for assignments ☐ Graphic organizers for subject areas ☐ Study guides for tests ☐ Voice reminders in watch or hand-held organizer ☐ Highlight notes to study for tests	Each teacher could talk into a tape recorder and give direction for assignments or upcoming tests. The small tape recorder might fit into Miki's agenda or notebook. The use of graphic organizers and study guides would help Miki identify important information for tests.
Attention/on-task behavior	☐ Preferential seating ☐ Study carrel ☐ Beeper or vibrating buzzer to cue on-task behavior ☐ PowerPoint or multimedia presentations in class	Attentional problems can be addressed by seating Miki away from distractions during independent work. Seating her in the front of the oom during lectures might also help her maintain attention. A vibrating buzzer could also be worn. When the buzzer goes off, it cues the student to be on task. This form of cognitive behavior management would make Miki more aware of her on-task behavior. Multimedia presentations involve text, graphics, video, etc. These presentations tend to be more motivating and maintain student attention.

The group discussed the options and decided to try several. Miki liked the idea of an organization notebook, taped assignment directions, a hand-held organizer, a modified keyboard, and speech-to-print software allowing her to talk into the computer and get a printed document. She didn't like the attention vibrator but agreed to try it for one month. Amelia Taylor allowed Miki to borrow the devices that were high tech, such as the hand-held organizer, speech-to-text software, modified keyboard, and vibrating buzzer, from the assistive technology center. Mary Paulovich agreed to make an agenda notebook for Miki and to get a hand-held tape recorder. She would also get a study carrel for her class and order the textbooks on tape. Starla Wright would talk to the other general education content teachers about videos, graphic organizers, and study guides and about using PowerPoint or multimedia presentations. The group also decided to meet again in one month to evaluate the usefulness of each device. This would allow Miki to try out things to see if they fit her needs.

Case Study Framework Questions

1. What makes this an exemplar case?
2. How do emotions influence behaviors in the main characters?
3. How is the factual information consistent with current professional literature?
4. Are issues oversimplified? If so, how?
5. Are people stereotyped? If so, how?
6. Discuss teacher dispositions that could facilitate interaction (i.e., self-reflection, tolerance for others, collaboration, multiple perspectives, sound ethical judgment, motivation to work with students with a variety of needs, capacity for advocacy) or that could become a barrier to working with the student discussed in the case.

Thinking Critically About the Case

1. What is assistive technology, and how can it help Miki succeed in the general education curriculum?
2. Describe the collaboration that took place at the meeting. Who was at the meeting, and what were their roles during the meeting?
3. Where do you think most students with mild cognitive disabilities are placed? What does the professional literature say about placement options for students with mild cognitive disabilities?

4. What additional modifications and adaptations (with and without technology) would be appropriate to help Miki succeed in this inclusive environment?

Activity

Look up information on assistive technology on the Internet. Categorize the devices Amelia Taylor suggested into the categories of No Tech, Low Tech, and High Tech. Add any new types of assistive technology you think might be appropriate for Miki.

RESOURCES FOR FURTHER INVESTIGATION

Print

Cuskelly, M., & Bryde, R. (2004). Attitudes towards the sexuality of adults with intellectual disabilities: Parents, support staff, and a community sample. *Journal of Intellectual and Developmental Disability, 29*(3), 255–265.

Taylor, R. L., Brady, M., & Richards, S. B. (2005). *Mental retardation: Historical perspectives, current practices, and future directions.* Boston: Allyn and Bacon.

Turnbull, A., & Turnbull, R. (2001). Self-determination for individuals with significant cognitive disabilities and their families. *Journal of the Association for Persons with Severe Handicaps, 26*(1), 56–62.

Tyne, A. (2004). The future of children with significant impairments: What parents fear and want, and what they and others may be able to do about it. *Mental Retardation, 42*(4), 315–317.

Vash, C. L. (2004). *Psychology of disability* (2nd ed.). New York: Springer.

Ward, K. M., Pfeiffer, K. T., & Trigler, J. S. (February 2001). Community services, issues, and service gaps for individuals with developmental disabilities who exhibit inappropriate sexual behaviors. *Mental Retardation, 39*(1), 11–19.

Wehmeyer, M. L., & Palmer, S. B. (2003). Adult outcomes for students with cognitive disabilities three years after high school: The impact of self-determination. *Education and Training in Developmental Disabilities, 38*(2), 131–144.

Zuna, N., & McDougall, D. (2004). Using positive behavior supports to manage avoidance of academic tasks. *Teaching Exceptional Children, 37*(1), 18–25.

Web

Internet Resource for Special Children
http://www.irsc.org

National Dissemination Center for Children with Disabilities
http://nichcy.org/index.html

Chapter 5

Cases Involving Students with Learning Disabilities

Case 1 "Benjamin"

Type of Case: Contemplation

Age Level: Elementary School

Characters

Benjamin Shea, second-grade boy diagnosed with a learning disability

Molly Shea, Benjamin's mother and a sixth-grade teacher

Brandi Keller, Benjamin's special education teacher

I've been a teacher for thirteen years now and have enjoyed my job. I've always thought of myself as a good teacher, but I think having children of my own has made me a better teacher. I now understand how difficult it is to trust someone else with your child. At first, the thought of having someone else look at, judge, and evaluate my child through eyes not tinted with love and affection was frightening. However, my first child, Emma, went to kindergarten ready to learn and explore. She fit in immediately and made all of my worries disappear. By first grade, she was reading small books independently and learning double-digit addition. This may have made it more difficult when my youngest child, Benjamin, had difficulty at school.

My husband and I knew that Benjamin was different from his sister. He reached most of his developmental milestones a little later, especially in the area of language. But people say not to compare your kids. Plus, he was more interested in physical activity. He would rather play with blocks and trains than sit and listen to me read or recite nursery rhymes. However, we always knew Benjamin was bright. Although he talked a little later than his sister, he still had an extensive vocabulary. We provided him with experiences at museums and through travel that advanced his vocabulary beyond that of his peers. He was curious about everything and had an excellent memory. Everyone talked about how much Benjamin knew about dinosaurs, magnets, sharks, weather, and the many other facts he had memorized.

As a mother, I noticed he had a lot of errors in word pronunciation. He substituted *w* for *l* long after other children his age. But it was so cute to hear him say, "I wuv you" or "I wike dat." When he entered kindergarten he couldn't sing the ABC song yet and knew none of his letter names. He couldn't write his name, and sometimes it was difficult for others to understand his speech.

Benjamin's kindergarten teacher was fantastic. I've always read to my children, but she taught Benjamin to love books. Her class was filled with books, and every week the students did activities centered on a particular book. She used all kinds of manipulatives and hands-on activities in both reading and math. After Christmas, the students began to keep a journal. Although Benjamin loved school, he wasn't keeping up with the other students. She recommended he work with the remedial reading teacher, and I began to worry.

After school, Benjamin and I would read together. I made flash cards for the alphabet. I got a phonics book. I bought computer games to teach early reading skills. I was so excited when he began to read. Then one day I noticed Benjamin didn't even look at the book as he read. He had memorized the entire book. He was using his excellent strength in memory to cover up the fact he wasn't learning. He had memorized the pictures on the flash cards to identify the letters. Anything we had done before, he knew. Anything new was almost impossible. I knew we were in trouble.

In first grade, Benjamin began to give up easily and become more distractible. My husband and I decided to have Benjamin tutored after school, and he continued seeing the remedial reading teacher. Benjamin became more and more frustrated at school. Although math was his strength, I could see the reading failure dragging down his self-esteem. He began to lose his sparkle at school. He complained about going to school and often said he felt sick. By the middle of first grade, his teacher suggested we have Benjamin evaluated for a learning disability.

I've had a lot of students in my class with a learning disability. Some I thought had genuine problems, and others I thought were just lazy. It was hard to believe my intelligent, creative, and wonderful little boy might have a disability. My husband and I agreed to start the preassessment process with the understanding that we might not agree to an evaluation.

The preassessment activities included modifications made in the general education classroom geared to Benjamin's needs. They included a reading buddy, classwide peer tutoring for sight words, remedial reading, extra time to complete reading assignments, books on tape, small-group instruction, computer software to reinforce phonics skills, and a shorter list of spelling words. The preassessment lasted four months, which seemed to take forever. By the end of the first grade, Benjamin was feeling more successful at school, but he wasn't catching up. In fact, as the other students accelerated in reading, he got farther behind. We decided to have him evaluated for special services and consented to a comprehensive evaluation.

The evaluation took place in June just before school was out. My husband and I went to the assessment meeting. There we found out that Benjamin had a problem with phonemic awareness. Although his hearing was fine, he had difficulty processing sounds. He couldn't tell the difference in words like *pen* and *pin*. He confused sounds like /g/ and /k/. Rhyming was almost impossible for him. Because he couldn't recognize and manipulate sounds, he couldn't associate the sounds with the letters. He didn't understand phonics.

Benjamin was diagnosed with an average to above-average intelligence and a deficit in reading. We agreed to the label of a specific learning disability and placement in a resource or pullout special education program for reading. At the beginning of second grade, Benjamin would begin seeing the special education teacher for 45 minutes a day to work specifically on phonemic awareness and reading. After the meeting and the Individualized Education Plan, my husband and I felt better. It was like being able to put a name to a problem, and the teachers were optimistic about Benjamin's progress given his higher IQ.

▶▶ Questions to Ponder

▶ Whose story is this?

▶ What is my background or previous experience with the issues presented in this case?

▶ What facts are presented?

▶ What opinions are presented?

The beginning of the school year started well. Benjamin looked forward to school every day. He loved the special education teacher and the classroom. He felt successful at school and enjoyed the activities in the special education class. His teacher did a lot of literature-based instruction, which Benjamin enjoyed. In November, I got a note requesting a parent-teacher conference. I have done many parent-teacher conferences, and I was expecting a 15-minute meeting to discuss Benjamin's grades and progress. I was unprepared for the meeting.

I entered the room to find both Benjamin's second-grade teacher and his special education teacher, Brandi Keller, sitting at a table. The second-grade teacher gave me Benjamin's report card. He had satisfactory grades in everything, with an S+ (satisfactory +) in math. The behavior sheet indicated that he was distractible and had difficulty following directions. Then Brandi Keller handed me a piece of paper addressing his IEP goals.

She went through each goal, talking about Benjamin's deficits in phonemic awareness and associative word learning, his weakness in memory for letters, words, and sounds. She explained he was reading on a primer level, which is associated with kindergarten, although he is in second grade. Miss Keller talked about how Benjamin would overrely on his background of knowledge when reading. He tended to "make up" the story instead of reading the story. She described his awkward pencil grasp, his poor fine motor control, and his rigidity for learning. She talked about how he memorized information and used it in rote ways instead of generalizing and applying it. She talked about his distractibility, his difficulty following oral and written directions, and his poor attention span. At one point, as she flipped through the testing reports done in first grade, she commented, "Wow, he scored a 128 on his IQ test. He must have had a good day." I didn't know what to say. What did that mean?

She went on to say that he had met none of his goals and was making slow progress. The teacher then told me she was happy Benjamin had been diagnosed with a learning disability so he could receive the support he needed. She felt 45 minutes a day of special education services was appropriate but would keep me updated. If he needed more time later in the year, we might amend the IEP.

I left the 40-minute meeting in a daze. I felt overwhelmed. On the way home, I cried in the car. What could I do? Why wasn't Benjamin making better progress? Did he have an attention deficit disorder? The teacher described him as being a rigid learner who relied on rote memory. She even questioned his IQ score.

She didn't tell me he was a bright little boy, eager to learn, who enjoyed school. I expected those comments. She forgot to say he had an excellent memory for facts, and he was curious and inquisitive. It seemed as though all of his strengths were overlooked or turned into weaknesses. What would I tell Benjamin about the meeting? He would want to know what his teacher had said.

The further I drove, the more I began to think the system had set me up for disappointment. IEPs are meant to document student weaknesses. Three months is not going to fix all of Benjamin's weaknesses. His teacher was just relating the facts to me, even if she did it in a very insensitive way. She was following the law by informing me about Benjamin's progress. But how could he feel so positive about school, and I feel so negative about it? I decided the answer was in a phrase used by the special education teacher in my building, "strengths-based assessment and IEP process." I was going to learn more about this. As I pulled in my driveway and saw Benjamin (my sweet, wonderful son) waiting for me, I wondered, how had I performed at parent-teacher conferences? How many parents had I talked to about their child and pointed out all of their deficiencies without regard to their unique capabilities and gifts? If I had done that, I would certainly never do it again.

Case Study Framework Questions

1. What makes this a contemplation case?
2. How do emotions influence behaviors in the main characters?
3. How is the factual information consistent with current professional literature?
4. Are issues oversimplified? If so, how?
5. Are people stereotyped? If so, how?
6. Discuss teacher dispositions that could facilitate interaction (i.e., self-reflection, tolerance for others, collaboration, multiple perspectives, sound ethical judgment, motivation to work with students with a variety of needs, capacity for advocacy) or that could become a barrier to working with the student discussed in the case.

Thinking Critically About the Case

1. Describe Benjamin, including both weaknesses and strengths.
2. What did Molly Shea mean when she said the system set her up for disappointment?
3. What could Benjamin's teacher have done differently during the meeting?
4. Where could you get more information on strengths-based assessment and planning?

Activity

Take the role of Brandi Keller and write or role-play her response to this case. Pretend she has just read the case. How would she respond?

CASE 2 "Duncan"

Type of Case: **Exemplar and Contemplation**
Age Level: **High School**

Characters

Duncan Ebeler, eleventh-grade student who has a learning disability

Griffin Nagel, eleventh-grade special education career/vocation teacher

Patricia Cywinski, owner of a fast food restaurant where
  Duncan is employed

"Griff, I'm not sure what I should do with Duncan," said Patricia Cywinski early one morning as they shared coffee during their monthly transition conference. "I've employed dozens of students from your program over the past ten years, and none have been such a challenge. You know how committed I am to this program. Having a grand-daughter with a significant disability has made me very aware of quality of life and independence issues for students with special needs. The sad part about the situation is that it's not Duncan's functioning skills. He's bright. His reading is exceptional. Math is weaker, of course, but he can take orders, handle money, count change when it's calculated on the cash register, and run the cash register. I have noticed that when a customer gives him additional money after the first payment has been entered into the register, and he must get exact change, he can't calculate the change in his head. He also has difficulty with telling time and reading the work schedule. But the big thing is that his mouth keeps getting him into trouble."

"Patricia, I can hear the frustration in your voice. Why don't you give me specific examples of what Duncan is doing?" said Griffin Nagel, Duncan's career/vocational teacher.

"Well, I could tell Duncan was going to be a challenge immediately. Last spring, when we were all meeting, we were doing an activity with the group where you draw circles on the board. In the center circle was the student's name. The next circle contained the names of close family and friends, then friends who aren't considered close. Finally, the last circle contained people who are paid to provide services, like a speech/language pathologist or an occupational therapist. The three students I employ were busy putting names or pictures into the circles to identify their support network. When I looked over at Duncan's paper, he had written the names Trixy, Babbett, and Mrs. Cywinski on the outer circle. He then announced in a loud voice, "I'd like to tell about the services I receive from Trixy." I went over to him and told him this was inappropriate. He didn't seem embarrassed. He just laughed and erased the names. After the meeting, I pulled him aside and told him I was his employer, and he needed to show me respect. Putting my name down as a joke was not funny, and he should be careful if he wanted to continue his employment."

"Wow Patricia, I had no idea he did that," said Griffin. "You handled it very well, but you should have told me. Maybe I could have also talked with Duncan to get the message across."

"I think you are right, Griff. I should have said something to you right then. Instead, I thought I could handle the situation. To Duncan's benefit, he hasn't said anything else inappropriate about me. He has just continued to say or do things that make the other employees and customers uncomfortable. I believe he thinks he is funny. I don't even think he knows that the other employees, especially the young women, dislike him."

"I know you have brought up the issue of inappropriate social skills and interactions to me before regarding Duncan. I have talked with him on several occasions about professional interactions. What other things has he said or done?" asked Griffin.

"Last month he reprogrammed Lyle's assistive technology communication board to say "spank you" instead of "thank you." He often stands too close to customers and tells them he has a learning disability and dyscalculia. They don't know how to respond. Anytime he gets an order wrong he blames it on his learning disability. We have a young woman named Kat who works with Duncan occasionally. She has asked not to be on the same shift with Duncan. He calls her kitty, and pets her. She told him to quit, but he thinks it's funny. The manager is always correcting him on his verbal exchange with people. When he asks someone if they want fries, and they say no, he says, "I'm used to women telling me no." The last straw came when I overheard him tell one of the girls, after closing last week, that he needed to go home and shoot something. I asked him what he meant by that remark, and he told me he needed to do some practice shooting. Don't get me wrong. I don't think Duncan is dangerous. He's just unaware his comments are inappropriate. I think he is looking for attention."

> ▶▶ **Questions to Ponder**
>
> ▶ Whose story is this?
>
> ▶ What is my background or previous experience with the issues presented in this case?
>
> ▶ What facts are presented?
>
> ▶ What opinions are presented?

"Patricia, I want you to know I am here to support you," stated Griffin. "Unfortunately, I haven't seen this type of behavior from Duncan at school. Of course, I only have him for the first period of the day, and my biggest challenge is getting him to stay awake. He is usually very quiet and tries to sleep for most of the period. I know he isn't well liked by the students in my class, but I'm not sure why. Since I am his case manager, I will check with his other teachers on a regular basis. He is in general education for all his classes. Because of his learning disability in math, he is in a basic math class. His teachers say academically he is doing pretty well, although math is difficult. He is passing all of his classes. They have reported that he appears immature. One teacher asked me to talk with him, because he was dancing around in the hall and pretending to strip. When I talked to him, he said he was just joking with his friends and wouldn't do it again. I think I just assumed because he is bright and his disability isn't as severe as some of my other students, he would do well in the work setting. I know how important social skills are to the work environment, but I don't see Duncan as having major social skills issues at school."

"I wonder why this isn't an issue at school," Patricia said.

"I don't know," said Griffin. "Maybe Duncan is trying to impress someone here. Maybe he feels more secure here because there isn't a lot of reading involved. I know he appears lethargic in my class. He says he stays up late at night playing video games and surfing the Net."

"Maybe it's a gender issue," said Patricia. "All my managers are female. Are his teachers male or female?"

"Most of his teachers are male. I don't know. I do know Duncan is having trouble at home. His parents divorced several years ago, and he lives with his mother. She told me in the last IEP meeting that he is often difficult to discipline at home, and she was thinking about sending Duncan to live with his father," stated Griffin.

"Griff, I am worried Duncan is going to get out of school and go from job to job because of his behavior. And he is a liability for a sexual harassment situation," said Patricia.

"Do you want me to find him another work placement, Patricia?" asked Griffin.

"No. I'm willing to work with Duncan. He has some very good traits. He is dependable. I personally don't like him, but I want to give him a chance. He just rubs me the wrong way. What can we do?" asked Patricia.

"Well, I'm pleased you are not giving up on him, Patricia. The social worker has a social skills group. I can try to get him into that group. They talk about a lot of issues such as talking to the opposite sex, respecting authority, making friends, accepting corrective feedback, etc. It's been really successful. My friend, Kirsten Bruce, runs the program, and she is really good with the kids. Then, I think we should talk to Duncan and spell this all out to him. He needs to know everything. Why don't you write everything down you just told me, and we can go over it with him. He needs to know the situation is serious, and he is at risk of losing his job here."

Griffin Nagel and Patricia Cywinski sat down with Duncan the next day and talked with him about his behavior. They explained their concerns about his behavior and how it could be thought of as harassing at times and disrespectful of others. They talked about their desire to help him fit in and be accepted by the other workers. Griffin listed Duncan's strengths and discussed how these strengths could be used in the work situation. They also explained the social skills training program. Duncan sat very quietly. He appeared angry. He didn't remember all the incidences and told Griffin and Patricia he had a different or an offbeat sense of humor. Two hours after the meeting, Patricia got this e-mail message from Duncan:

Dear Mrs. Cywinski,

It was shocking to see what you wrote about me to my teacher. You never expressed any extreme dislike for me at work. You talked about respectful behavior in your letter, where is my respect? You could have discussed my flaws with me so I could work on fixing them. But you decided to play with my life and talk to my teacher behind my back. Was that respectful? THINK ABOUT IT!!!! You have an attitude of being better than everyone else. Gina told me you don't like her and are always on her case. Why don't you show some respect to her? I know it seems like I'm bashing you, but what do you expect of me when you tried to get me in trouble at school because you couldn't open your mouth and talk to me? I just thought you should be analyzed too. I'm sorry all of this happened and I'm sorry you can't realize that your way isn't the only way.

Sincerely,
Duncan Ebeler

Case Study Framework Questions

1. What makes this an exemplar and contemplation case?
2. How do emotions influence behaviors in the main characters?
3. How is the factual information consistent with current professional literature?
4. Are issues oversimplified? If so, how?
5. Are people stereotyped? If so, how?
6. Discuss teacher dispositions that could facilitate interaction (i.e., self-reflection, tolerance for others, collaboration, multiple perspectives, sound ethical judgment, motivation to work with students with a variety of needs, capacity for advocacy) or that could become a barrier to working with the student discussed in the case.

Thinking Critically About the Case

1. What should Patricia Cywinski do now? Could she have done anything to prevent this situation from occurring?
2. What do you think Duncan is most upset about?
3. Did Griffin Nagel violate issues of confidentiality when he talked to Patricia Cywinski about Duncan's academic performance and home life? Why or why not?
4. What is dyscalculia?
5. What does the professional literature say about learning disabilities and social skills?

Activity

Complete this critical incident questionnaire.

- While you were reading the case, at what moment did you feel most engaged in what was happening?
- While you were reading the case, at what moment did you feel most disengaged from what was happening?
- What action in the case did you most identify with?
- What action in the case made you confused or puzzled?
- What surprised you most in the case?
- Have you ever made a social error? How did you solve the situation?

RESOURCES FOR FURTHER INVESTIGATION

Print

Anderson, S. A. (2000, Summer). How parental involvement makes a difference in reading achievement. *Reading Improvement, 37*(2), 61–86.

Bender, W. N. (2004). *Learning disabilities: Characteristics, identification, and teaching strategies* (5th ed.). Boston: Pearson/Allyn and Bacon.

Court, D., & Givon, S. (2003). Group intervention: Improving social skills of adolescents with learning disabilities. *Teaching Exceptional Children, 36*(2), 50–55.

Honig, B. (2001). *Teaching our children to read: The components of an effective, comprehensive reading program* (2nd ed.). Thousand Oaks, CA: Corwin.

Irving Belson, S. (2003). *Technology for exceptional learners.* Boston: Houghton Mifflin.

Lerner, J. W. (2003). *Learning disabilities.* Boston: Houghton Mifflin.

Scott, V. G. (2005). *Phonological awareness: Ready to use lessons, games, and activities.* Minnetonka, MN: Peytral.

Web

Closing the Gap
http://www.closingthegap.com

LD Online
http://www.ldonline.org

National Center for Learning Disabilities
http://www.ncld.org

Nonverbal Learning Disorder
http://www.nldontheweb.org

Chapter **6**

Cases Involving Students with Emotional and Behavior Disorders

CASE 1 "Keesha"

Type of Case: Contemplation

Age Level: High School

Characters

    Keesha Hawkins, ninth-grade student with a disability

    Kevin Smith, science teacher

    Deanna Howard, special education teacher

    Carmen Diaz, principal

Kevin Smith had been a science teacher at Jamaica High School for twenty-eight years. Kevin taught five classes with about twenty-five students in each section. In the beginning of the year he was always busy, preparing labs, teaching safety rules, handing out textbooks, and so on. Generally, students were motivated and wanted to do well in his classes.

Kevin felt that the focus in his class was to provide experiences that students would need to be successful in advanced courses within the high school science curriculum. He always made sure that his tests and labs were consistent with the types that students would experience in other classes and in college. He was aware of various programs offered to students with disabilities, and he occasionally had students with mild disabilities placed in his classes. Regardless of the student's ability, Kevin treated all students the same and expected exactly the same work from each student. He made no accommodations for students with special needs. He felt that he didn't have the time and believed that any services or modifications were the responsibility of the special education staff because the students belonged to them. The special education department often sent a teacher's aide into his classes when students with disabilities were assigned. Kevin theorized that, without the aide, students with disabilities would get no help because, he said, "If I made the help available to them myself, I would have too many special students placed in my classes," and the result might be adjustments to his curriculum. Kevin felt that all classes at the high school level were becoming "watered down" as teachers were being forced to deal with the needs of all students.

Kevin was known as an excellent teacher with high standards. In fact, students at Jamaica did well on the state test in science, and they generally did well in advanced high school science, partly because of Kevin's science program. On this particular Friday, Kevin reached in his mailbox to find a "Communication Form" addressed to him. The form included the following information about a ninth-grade student named Keesha.

COMMUNICATION FORM
CONFIDENTIAL

Student Name: Keesha Hawkings   **Grade:** 9   **Semester:** 1

Student's Disability: Social and Emotional Disorder

Student's Special Needs: Keesha has been diagnosed with obsessive-compulsive disorder (OCD) and is under the care of a psychiatrist. She receives all instruction in the regular education classroom with supplementary aids and services provided by the special education teacher and/or aide. She has superior intelligence and reads at the twelfth-grade level. Her OCD manifests itself in the classroom in the area of handwriting. She retraces each stroke of the letter to eliminate corners until the paper is torn.

Adaptations and Accommodations Needed in the Regular Classroom:

_____ Use of audiocassette

_____ Use of tests in large print or Braille

_____ Use of calculators _____

__X__ Use of other assistive devices: Keesha should use a computer for written tasks as much as possible; a laptop computer is available for Keesha.

_____ Modification of classroom _____

__X__ Modification of time allowed: Keesha needs extended time during tests.

_____ Tests orally read _____

__X__ Other: Keesha should use a student note taker when taking notes. Please select a student in Keesha's class who takes adequate notes. Special note-taking paper will be provided for the student note taker.

During tests or other written work such as worksheets, the teacher's assistant from special education will come to class and assist. Please contact the special education teacher at least one day in advance to schedule the teacher's assistant.

Contact Person for Assistance: Deanna Howard, special education teacher

Notes: I'm sorry you were unable to attend Keesha's IEP meeting last week! I would like to meet with you in the next few weeks to discuss Keesha's progress. Keesha's IEP is available for review in my office.

Deanna

▶▶ **Questions to Ponder**

▶ Whose story is this?

▶ What is my background or previous experience with the issues presented in this case?

▶ What facts are presented?

▶ What opinions are presented?

Kevin quickly read through the form and placed it in the back of his grade book as he walked briskly to his next class. He wondered to himself why a student who was so bright and capable would need any special education assistance. He decided that he would talk to the special education teacher after having Keesha in class for a few weeks.

Keesha sat in the front row during Kevin's third-hour science class. After Kevin had spent several days going over expectations for his class and handing out books, he was ready to introduce a lesson on space. Kevin began to ask questions to students to quickly assess their knowledge and arouse their interest in space. He then began a short lecture on the solar system. After the lecture, he handed out a worksheet with questions that went along with chapter 1 in the text. He directed students to use the remainder of the hour to read the chapter and answer the questions. Students began to quietly work. Keesha also got out a pencil, opened her book, and began reading. After about five minutes, Kevin noticed that Keesha was trying to erase her answers. After erasing, she began to write again. This process continued until her paper tore from the continual erasing and writing. Her face was red and her eyes were teary. The bell rang and Keesha quickly walked out of the room.

The next day Kevin showed a video and reminded the class that they would have a quiz over the first section of chapter 1 the following day. Keesha sat quietly and listened. He reminded students that they should study their notes and the worksheet that they completed.

On the third day, Kevin handed out the quiz, which consisted of ten short-answer questions. Keesha again began writing and erasing again and again. Kevin could tell that she was frustrated, and he called her up to his desk. He asked her what was wrong, and she said she couldn't write the answers to the questions. Kevin said she should know the answers, and if she didn't, she should have studied more. He sent Keesha back to her desk, where she quietly began to write again. When papers were collected, Kevin noted that Keesha's paper had been worn through after the first question and that the other questions were blank. While students were previewing the next section in the chapter, Kevin graded the quizzes and put a red "F" on Keesha's quiz.

That afternoon, as Kevin was cleaning up after a lab at the end of the day, Deanna Howard walked into his room. She asked if she could talk to him for a few minutes about Keesha.

DEANNA: Kevin, Keesha Hawkins came to my room today in tears about failing a quiz in your third-hour class. She really needs help with her writing. On the communication form I left in your mailbox, I indicated that you needed to let me know when written work would be required and I would schedule the teacher's aide into your class to help her. She also needs help taking notes. I have special paper, and if you will select a student to write notes on the paper, the student only needs to tear off a copy for Keesha.

KEVIN: Deanna, you know how I feel about having your students in my classes. I will take them, but they have to do the same work as everyone else. It's only fair. I can tell that Keesha is very bright, so she should be able to compensate.

DEANNA: Kevin, Keesha's emotional status is rather fragile now, especially after failing and being unable to take notes in your class.

KEVIN: Well, that's not my concern. If you think she can't handle the class, just pull her and put her in special education.

Deanna quickly became frustrated with the conversation and walked out of the classroom. Kevin continued cleaning the lab. Deanna went directly to Carmen Diaz, the building principal, and explained the situation. Although Carmen was sympathetic, she was reluctant to confront Kevin. Deanna was upset with the situation and knew she had to do something to help Keesha. After reviewing the schedule, she made a schedule change to place Keesha in a general science class the same hour with a general education teacher who worked well with students who had disabilities. Although Keesha could have succeeded in the biology class, at least in the general science class she would have the accommodations she needed.

Case Study Framework Questions

1. What makes this a contemplation case?
2. How do emotions influence behaviors in the main characters?
3. How is the factual information consistent with current professional literature?

4. Are issues oversimplified? If so, how?
5. Are people stereotyped? If so, how?
6. Discuss teacher dispositions that facilitate interaction (i.e., self-reflection, tolerance for others, collaboration, multiple perspectives, sound ethical judgment, motivation to work with students with a variety of needs, capacity for advocacy) or that could become a barrier to working with the student discussed in the case.

Thinking Critically About the Case

1. What strategies might Mr. Smith have used to accommodate Keesha?
2. Given the problem, describe the pros and cons to the solution.
3. If you were the special education teacher, how would you attempt to resolve the conflict with Mr. Smith? How could you, as special education teacher, ensure that Mr. Smith would follow the IEP?
4. What other professionals should be involved, and what should they be doing?

Activity

Choose the position of either Mr. Smith (who refuses to accommodate Keesha) or Ms. Howard (who thinks Keesha should be accommodated). Orally present this person's position to your partner or discussion group. Then orally present the other person's position. Compare and contrast both positions and speculate on how the conflict could be resolved.

CASE 2 "Adam"

Type of Case: **Contemplation and Exemplar**

Age Level: **Middle School**

Characters

Adam McClain, sixth-grade student with an emotional disability

Omar Muhammad, principal

Elise McClain, Adam's parent

Carlos Perez, social studies teacher

Mary Sims, special education teacher

Melissa Brooks, Adam's aunt

Note to the reader: You will read two different scenarios of the same IEP meeting. As you read each scenario, focus on the extent to which the parent is a partner in the meeting.

Scenario 1

Ms. SIMS: Good morning. The purpose of the meeting today is to review Adam's IEP and develop an IEP for next year. First, I would like everyone to introduce himself or herself. Please state your name and your position. I will begin. I am Mary Sims. I am Adam's special education teacher.

MR. MUHAMMAD: I'm Omar Muhammad. I'm the principal.

MR. PEREZ: I'm Mr. Perez. I'm Adam's social studies teacher.

Ms. McCLAIN: I'm Elise McClain, Adam's mother.

Ms. SIMS: Elise, we are going to talk about how Adam has progressed this year and make some recommendations on how to better address his disabilities next year. As the team knows, Adam has difficulty relating to peers and accepting the authority of adults. I know, Elise, that you have suggested that this may be due to previous abuse by Adam's natural parents before he was adopted. He is also somewhat impulsive. He reacts, and then is sorry for misbehaving upon reflection. Although he has made good progress, Adam benefits from special education.

Ms. McClain: OK.

Ms. Sims: I would like everyone to turn to page 3 of Adam's current IEP. We are going to review his progress on his goals. As you know, Elise, Adam is doing poorly in social studies. He is not passing tests or completing assignments correctly. In fact, he is failing. He disrupts the class every day by shouting out and refusing to complete the assigned work. He refused to take notes from the board and won't read the text or study for tests. Other students in the class are affected by Adam's behavior.

Mr. Perez: Adam is completely disrupting the teaching process. He seems to have no idea of what we are discussing, although he shouts out constantly. I feel that he is wasting his time and my time. It is a disservice to me and other students to allow him to stay in my class. In fact, he is just taking up space in the classroom. It is a waste. He really needs to go back to special education.

Ms. Sims: We think that Adam's learning would increase if he were in the special education classroom all day so that we could concentrate on his behavior rather than allowing him to continue to disrupt the social studies class.

Ms. McClain: I realize that Adam can be a challenge in class. However, he is very insecure and sensitive. He would be devastated if he were returned to the special education class. Is there some way that we can work with him so that he is successful in the social studies class? Maybe we could make up a behavior chart or something.

Ms. Sims: I am sorry, Ms. McClain. Adam is not benefiting to the extent that we expect in the regular education classroom. He will really do much better in special education. He just cannot stay in the social studies classroom.

Ms. McClain: I have had it with you people! You don't care what I think. You had your minds made up before I walked in the door!

Mr. Muhammad: We have to do what we feel is in the best interest of your child. You don't have to agree with us. I will be happy to discuss your rights with you, if you would like.

> ▶▶ **Questions to Ponder**
>
> ▶ Whose story is this?
>
> ▶ What is my background or previous experience with the issues presented in this case?
>
> ▶ What facts are presented?
>
> ▶ What opinions are presented?

Scenario 2

Ms. Sims: Good morning. Can I get anyone coffee? The purpose of the meeting today is to review Adam's IEP and develop a new IEP for next year. First, I would like everyone to introduce himself or herself. Please say your name and your position relative to Adam. Also, on the nametag, please write how you want to be addressed during this meeting. I will begin. I am Mary Sims. I am Adam's special education teacher. You can call me Mary.

Mr. Muhammad: I'm Mr. Omar Muhammad. I'm the principal. I would prefer to be called Mr. Muhammad.

Mr. Perez: I'm Carlos Perez. I'm Adam's social studies teacher. You can call me Carlos.

Ms. McClain: I'm Elise McClain, Adam's mother. You can call me Elise.

Ms. Brooks: I'm Melissa Brooks. I'm Adam's aunt. I am here just to listen. You can call me Melissa.

Ms. Sims: Elise, I spoke with you last week when we were setting up this meeting. I explained to you at that time that we would be talking about how Adam has done this year and would be making some recommendations on how to better address his abilities next year. I told you that we were thinking about providing more of his education in the special education classroom. You indicated to me that you would prefer that he remain in the general education classroom. In the past, Adam's IEP has focused on helping him develop positive peer relationships and accept adult authority. Adam has also worked on thinking before reacting in classroom situations.

Ms. McClain: I want you to know that I really appreciate your telephone call. No one has ever called me before a meeting to tell me what it is about or to ask me if I had any concerns. Your call makes me feel like I have input into Adam's education. I always came to these meetings with lots of anxiety because I didn't know what was going to happen. I have prioritized my goals for Adam as you suggested. I still have some anxiety, but I feel more a part of the team. I also appreciate being encouraged to bring someone with me for support. It's really hard to think in these meetings. It helps to have my sister here with me.

Ms. Sims: Thanks, Elise. We are trying to encourage parents to participate in IEP meetings without fear that they are going to be surprised by something we may say. I would like to begin the meeting by going around the room and asking each of you to tell the group about some of Adam's strengths or abilities. I'll start. Adam has a good sense of humor. He is friendly and knows everyone's name. He is courteous to me.

Mr. Muhammad: I'm really proud of Adam. I see him walking into the cafeteria with some of the other boys in his grade level. They are talking and seem to be getting along.

Mr. Perez: Adam turned in his assignment on the Civil War. He was able to name some of the battles and tell about their results. He really enjoyed drawing the flags.

Ms. McClain: Adam usually brings home his homework and almost always completes it with just some assistance from me.

Ms. Brooks: Adam is a good boy. He enjoys playing with his cousins.

Ms. Sims: Thank you. I would like for everyone to look at page 3 of Adam's current IEP. We are going to review his progress. When Adam is interested in a subject, he seems to attend to his work and wants to complete projects. When Adam is not interested in a topic, he has difficulty attending.

Mr. Perez: I can tell that Adam does like to be in my class. He jokes around with some of the other boys before class begins. Sometimes when I ask the class a question, Adam shouts out an answer that doesn't go with the topic at hand and other kids laugh. I also wonder if sometimes the reading is difficult for him, because he is reluctant to complete all the work assigned. Maybe I could give him a copy of the class notes before class so that he wouldn't have to write everything during class.

Ms. Sims: If you could give me the notes and assignments in advance, I could help Adam read the information in advance. Maybe he could answer questions and would feel able to complete the work. I could also check with him at the end of the day to make sure he has written all assignments in his notebook. I also wonder if we may need to develop a behavior sheet with Adam and reward him for paying attention in class and using class time appropriately to complete assignments.

Ms. McClain: That would be wonderful! Adam really wants to stay in social studies. Wow, this meeting is turning out better than I thought it would. I really appreciate your willingness to make some changes to accommodate Adam.

Case Study Framework Questions

1. What makes this case both a contemplation and exemplar case?
2. How do emotions influence behaviors in the main characters?
3. How is the factual information consistent with current professional literature?
4. Are issues oversimplified? If so, how?
5. Are people stereotyped? If so, how?
6. Discuss teacher dispositions that could facilitate interaction (i.e., self-reflection, tolerance for others, collaboration, multiple perspectives, sound ethical judgment, motivation to work with students with a variety of needs, capacity for advocacy) or that could become a barrier to working with the student discussed in the case.

Thinking Critically About the Case

1. How were these two scenarios different? Complete the chart on the next page.

Issue	Scenario 1	Scenario 2
Focus of meeting: strengths, weaknesses		
Decisions made: placement in general vs. special education		
Parent input: how much, how it was regarded		
Parent preparation for meeting		
General educator's willingness to accommodate Adam		

2. In the first meeting, the parent doesn't really have an opportunity to participate. Why not?
3. Why is it important for parents to be prepared for an IEP meeting?

Activity

One important skill that facilitates the discussion of a child's strengths (as opposed to weaknesses) is reframing. In reframing, the child is described as a person with skills, gifts, and capacities, rather than as a child with problems, deficits, and labels. For example, some professionals talk about "dysfunctional" families, "emotionally disturbed" children, or "mentally impaired" children. Read the following descriptions of a sixth-grade child who has been placed in a self-contained classroom for children with emotional disturbance. For every term, brainstorm several terms that focus on strengths instead of weaknesses. The first two have been completed for you as examples.

Deficits-Based Descriptors	Strengths-Based Descriptors
Aggressive behavior	Assertive, expressing self, advocating for himself, standing up for himself
Skipping class	Independent, prioritizing needs, avoiding stress
Cursing	
Hitting	
Stealing	
Refusing to complete work	
Lying	

How can the strengths-based descriptors be used to facilitate an IEP meeting?

RESOURCES FOR FURTHER INVESTIGATION

Print

Frey, K. S., Hirschstein, M. K., & Guzzo, B. A. (2000). Second step: Preventing aggression by promoting social competence. *Journal of Emotional and Behavioral Disorders, 8,* 102–112.

Kauffman, J. M. (2001). *Characteristics of emotional and behavioral disorders of children* (7th ed.). Columbus, OH: Merrill/Prentice-Hall.

Lewis, T. J., & Sugai, G. (1999). Effective behavior support: A systems approach to proactive schoolwide management. *Focus on Exceptional Children, 21*(6), 1–24.

Metzler, C. W., Biglan, A., Rusby, J. C., & Sprague, J. R. (2001). Evaluation of a comprehensive behavior management program to improve school-wide positive behavior support. *Education and Treatment of Children, 24,* 448–479.

Web

American Academy of Child and Adolescent Psychiatry
http://www.aacap.org

Council for Children with Behavioral Disorders
http://www.ccbd.net

National Mental Health Association
http://www.nmha.org

Chapter 7

Cases Involving Students with Communication Disorders

CASE 1 "Kerim"

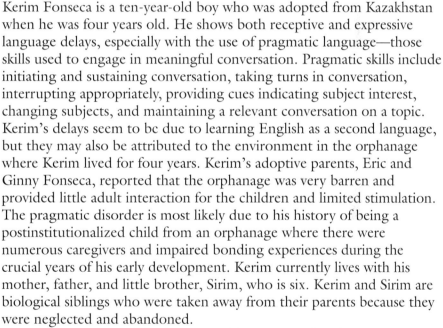

Type of Case: Exemplar

Age Level: Elementary School

Characters

Kerim Fonseca, ten-year-old boy

Eric and Ginny Fonseca, Kerim's parents

Kerim Fonseca is a ten-year-old boy who was adopted from Kazakhstan when he was four years old. He shows both receptive and expressive language delays, especially with the use of pragmatic language—those skills used to engage in meaningful conversation. Pragmatic skills include initiating and sustaining conversation, taking turns in conversation, interrupting appropriately, providing cues indicating subject interest, changing subjects, and maintaining a relevant conversation on a topic. Kerim's delays seem to be due to learning English as a second language, but they may also be attributed to the environment in the orphanage where Kerim lived for four years. Kerim's adoptive parents, Eric and Ginny Fonseca, reported that the orphanage was very barren and provided little adult interaction for the children and limited stimulation. The pragmatic disorder is most likely due to his history of being a postinstitutionalized child from an orphanage where there were numerous caregivers and impaired bonding experiences during the crucial years of his early development. Kerim currently lives with his mother, father, and little brother, Sirim, who is six. Kerim and Sirim are biological siblings who were taken away from their parents because they were neglected and abandoned.

Kerim is very small for his age and began attending kindergarten at the age of seven. Before he attended public school, Kerim's mother, Ginny Fonseca, worked with the boys at home, and he received speech and language therapy from a private therapist. His medical history is limited because of his adoption. However, both Kerim and Sirim were treated for intestinal parasites and anemia upon entering the United States. Mr. and Mrs. Fonseca were initially most concerned about Kerim's possible health problems and less concerned with language and behavioral/emotional issues. However, they have identified communication and social problems to be the most troublesome problems for Kerim now.

Kerim has been given an intelligence test on two different occasions. His latest cognitive evaluation produced the scores of 72 verbal IQ, 81 performance IQ, and 75 full-scale IQ. Kerim was also evaluated for a central auditory processing disorder by an audiologist. The audiology evaluation, which involved pure tone testing and speech recognition, revealed a mild hearing loss. According to the results, Kerim is functioning at an auditory age of six years, seven months. He is currently receiving speech services in a group setting 20 minutes twice a week. He also receives services in special education in reading and written language in the general education classroom.

Kerim's initial behavioral problems included eating voraciously, making stereotyped movements (such as hand flapping and spinning), and withdrawing from his parents and brother. Most of these have disappeared; however, Kerim still has issues that concern his parents. The most striking is his inability to engage in a meaningful conversation with others. A language evaluation done by the speech and language pathologist indicates that Kerim has difficulty with pragmatic skills such as topicalization, planning what to say, giving information, and appropriately interrupting during discourse. These difficulties have led to significantly inappropriate social skills. Kerim does not understand the "unwritten" rules governing social interactions and fails to recognize the social constraints that are apparent to others. He chatters without being aware of the listener's interest or lack of interest, questions incessantly to initiate and maintain social contact, is overfriendly, wants to talk to strangers, and makes inappropriate comments that don't match the social situation that he is currently in. Kerim's diagnosed central auditory processing disorder also affects his pragmatic language. He in unable to organize "incoming" auditory information for easy recall or use to solve problems. His parents have also noticed this weakness and report that Kerim has poor reasoning and listening ability and an inability to attend to detail. They state that his communication difficulties have contributed to their feeling that Kerim has not developed a secure attachment relationship with them or other family members.

▶▶ **Questions to Ponder**

▶ Whose story is this?

▶ What is my background or previous experience with the issues presented in this case?

▶ What facts are presented?

▶ What opinions are presented?

Although Kerim is receiving special education services in speech/language and reading/language arts, his parents and teachers felt they needed to meet because Kerim has language weaknesses and significant dysfunction in central auditory processing and also because he is not making significant progress on his IEP goals and objectives. Kerim's parents, the general education teacher, the special education teacher, and the speech and language pathologist scheduled a meeting to discuss his needs. Mr. and Mrs. Fonseca want Kerim to continue receiving special education services in an inclusive setting with limited pullout services in special education. The team agreed to continue Kerim's current placement in general education with speech/language services in a group setting 20 minutes twice a week and class-within-a-class special education support in reading and written language in the general education classroom. In this model, the special education teacher coteaches reading and language arts with the general education teacher each day for 30 minutes. On the basis of their discussion of Kerim's strengths and educational concerns, the following recommendations were made for his classroom teacher:

1. Give Kerim preferential seating
2. Reduce environment noises such as fans, motors, or blowers
3. Recognize that he may have more difficulty than most students with dialects, scratched tapes, soft-spoken voices, and areas with reverberations
4. When presenting information:
   - Keep it simple
   - Use clear and moderately loud speech
   - Chunk information and use pauses
   - Periodically check by having Kerim paraphrase or summarize
   - Help him to monitor his own attention and focus during auditory presentation
   - Provide additional time to grasp direction, new concepts, and information
5. Use visual presentation of information
6. Teach Kerim to seek assistance when needed
7. Rephrase information when Kerim does not understand
8. Praise Kerim for looking and listening

After implementing the suggestions, Kerim's teachers and parents began to see limited improvement in Kerim's ability to function independently within the general education classroom. Although he continues to function below grade level in academics and continues to have difficulty with communication, the collaboration between the teachers and parents is allowing him to finish the school year without additional pullout time in special education. The team has decided to meet at the end of the year to discuss Kerim's future placement. The teachers are afraid that the advanced reading necessary in fourth grade will make Kerim less able to succeed in content areas such as science and social studies. His parents agree that Kerim may need additional support in the special education program next year. However, they are pleased with the teacher's willingness to work with him in the general education classroom this year.

Case Study Framework Questions

1. What makes this an exemplar case?
2. How do emotions influence behaviors in the main characters?
3. How is the factual information consistent with current professional literature?
4. Are issues oversimplified? If so, how?
5. Are people stereotyped? If so, how?
6. Discuss teacher dispositions that could facilitate interaction (i.e., self-reflection, tolerance for others, collaboration, multiple perspectives, sound ethical judgment, motivation to work with students with a variety of needs, capacity for advocacy) or that could become a barrier to working with the student discussed in the case.

Thinking Critically About the Case

1. What is pragmatic language, and how does it affect Kerim's social skills?
2. What are the two suggested causes for Kerim's communication disorder?
3. What have Kerim's teachers done to support his inclusion within the general education classroom?
4. Why are the teachers concerned about Kerim's placement for next year?

Activity

5-3-1 Activity: Get into small groups. Each individual writes five key words that capture the important issues in this case and then shares these words with his or her group. Then each group selects three words from among all the words offered as those that represent the three key issues. Using the three words, each group writes one sentence that summarizes the ideas presented in the case.

CASE 2 "Bradley"

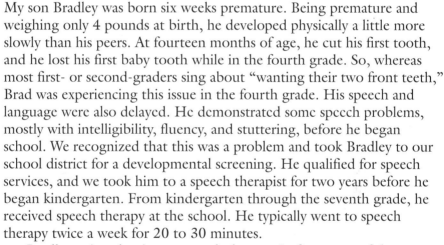

Type of Case: Exemplar

Age Level: Early Childhood to High School

Characters

Bradley Clark, twenty-one-year-old male who received speech services throughout school

Mike and Betty Clark, Bradley's father and mother

My son Bradley was born six weeks premature. Being premature and weighing only 4 pounds at birth, he developed physically a little more slowly than his peers. At fourteen months of age, he cut his first tooth, and he lost his first baby tooth while in the fourth grade. So, whereas most first- or second-graders sing about "wanting their two front teeth," Brad was experiencing this issue in the fourth grade. His speech and language were also delayed. He demonstrated some speech problems, mostly with intelligibility, fluency, and stuttering, before he began school. We recognized that this was a problem and took Bradley to our school district for a developmental screening. He qualified for speech services, and we took him to a speech therapist for two years before he began kindergarten. From kindergarten through the seventh grade, he received speech therapy at the school. He typically went to speech therapy twice a week for 20 to 30 minutes.

Bradley enjoyed going to speech therapy. In fact, most of the speech/language pathologists worked with Bradley's speech while playing games or working on something that interested him. They told us that there is no "cure" for stuttering. The best success comes when children get early intervention, before they learn that talking can be hard or they have negative experiences when talking. They also told us not to say things like "stop," "relax," or "slow down and think about what you are going to say." This often frustrates the child and can even trigger more stuttering. It's best to simply repeat back what the child says so he will know he is being understood. However, in the general education classroom, the teachers would often stop Bradley while he was talking in class and have him start back from the beginning. He said this would make him feel embarrassed and nervous, and he would do even worse. Because of this, Bradley was less likely to raise his hand in school or participate verbally in lessons. When asked questions in class, he would often say that he didn't know, just to avoid talking in front of the class. His speech difficulties also impacted his social development. Bradley tended to feel less self-confident and was less outgoing in school. When he was in elementary school, he was often worried the other students would make fun of him.

What did help Bradley was making him aware of his dysfluency (this happened during his speech therapy) and giving him strategies or tools to deal with it, such as using breathing techniques, practicing self-talk, and avoiding certain words that begin with letters or blends that trigger dysfluency or "lockups." The speech pathologists helped us work with Bradley at home by validating his feelings and praising or encouraging his effort. We were taught to validate his feelings by reflecting on what he said and probing him for more information. For instance, if Bradley said, "I hate talking in class," we would respond by saying, "You don't like talking in class. Tell me more about that." If he replied by saying, "I get into speech lockups, and the kids make fun of me," we would say, "That sounds frustrating. It's okay to feel angry about talking in class." This created an environment where Brad felt safe sharing his beliefs and feelings. The speech and language pathologists also taught us to praise Bradley using observations about his performance like "I noticed you are trying to talk more with the kids on the baseball team. It makes me proud when you try to do something new!"

▶▶ **Questions to Ponder**

▶ Whose story is this?

▶ What is my background or previous experience with the issues presented in this case?

▶ What facts are presented?

▶ What opinions are presented?

As my son matured, so did his speech. His speech became more intelligible, but the dysfluency remained. We moved to another state during the summer of his eighth-grade year. He wanted to try working on his fluency alone without the help of special education services. We supported his decision, and he went to school without any speech services. But, during his sophomore year in high school, I noticed that his dysfluency was not improving and asked him if he thought having speech services would help. He thought they would, and I asked the speech/language coordinator for the district what I needed to do to get speech services for him again. Bradley was evaluated for speech dysfluency through the school district and qualified for speech/language services. He received speech therapy every day until he graduated from high school.

While in high school, Bradley became interested in Spanish and French. He excelled in these classes and completed four years of French in three semesters as well as all classes offered in Spanish. During this time, he also worked with the English as a second language (ESL) program at the local preschool. He loved the children and felt very comfortable talking with them in their primary language. This experience built his confidence, and his fluency improved. It also got him interested in a career in education.

After graduation, Bradley went to Spain for seven months through the Rotary Club program and became fluent in Spanish. When he returned, he enrolled at a state university and will graduate in May with a degree in Spanish Education K–12 and an endorsement in ESL. In the last three years of college, Bradley worked at the Spanish radio station on campus. In addition to being fluent in Spanish, he is considered proficient in speaking French and emergent in speaking German. Interestingly, he says he has less difficulty with fluency when speaking Spanish and French because German and English have stronger consonants. Last summer, he taught English to businessmen from Costa Rica.

I guess you could say that speech is a weakness while language is a strength for Bradley. He has never allowed his dysfluency in speech to hinder or alter his goals. He is comfortable speaking in front of large groups about familiar topics and often does so to educate others on issues of dysfluency. Speaking spontaneously to people he doesn't know is still challenging, but he uses the strategies and tools he has learned to move through the moment and be successful in the conversation. He recently signed a contract to teach Spanish at a high school in a town not far from where he goes to college. His long-range goal is to acquire a doctorate degree and teach linguistics at a university. I have no doubt that he will achieve his goal.

Case Study Framework Questions

1. What makes this an exemplar case?
2. How do emotions influence behaviors in the main characters?
3. How is the factual information consistent with current professional literature?
4. Are issues oversimplified? If so, how?

5. Are people stereotyped? If so, how?
6. Discuss teacher dispositions that could facilitate interaction (i.e., self-reflection, tolerance for others, collaboration, multiple perspectives, sound ethical judgment, motivation to work with students with a variety of needs, capacity for advocacy) or that could become a barrier to working with the student discussed in the case.

Thinking Critically About the Case

1. How can emotions affect dysfluency in speech?
2. What did the speech/language pathologists do to help Bradley with his fluency issues?
3. What was not helpful when Bradley encountered a fluency problem?
4. How could you teach other students to support Bradley in his communication?

Activity

Rewrite the following conversation between parent and child to validate the child's feelings:

CHILD: "I don't want to stand up and do a book report in front of class."

PARENT: "You loved reading that book."

CHILD: "You know I will block and everyone will laugh."

PARENT: "Now that you are in fourth grade, you should expect to have to give book reports. It's part of getting older."

CHILD: "I'm not going to do it."

PARENT: "Then you aren't going to pass the assignment."

RESOURCES FOR FURTHER INVESTIGATION

Print

Ainswoth, S. (1995). *If your child stutters: A guide for parents.* Memphis: Stuttering Foundation of America.

Garcia, L. J., Laroche, C., & Barrette, J. (2002). Work integration issues go beyond the nature of the communication disorder. *Journal of Communication Disorders, 35*(2), 187–211.

Masters, M. G., Stecker, N. A., & Katz, J. (1998). *Central auditory processing disorders: Mostly management.* Needham Heights, MA: Allyn and Bacon.

Reed, V. A. (2005). *Introduction to children with language disorders.* Boston: Allyn and Bacon.

Richard, G. J. (2001). *The source for processing disorders.* East Moline, IL: LinguiSystems.

Web

American Speech-Language-Hearing Association
http://www.asha.org

Central Auditory Processing Disorder Parents' Page
http://pages.cthome.net/cbristol/capd.html

National Stuttering Association
http://www.nsastutter.org

Chapter 8

Cases Involving Students Who Are Deaf or Hard of Hearing

CASE 1 "James"

Type of Case: **Exemplar**

Age Level: **High School**

Characters

James Jackson, sixteen-year-old student with severe hearing impairment

George Jackson, James's father

Jennifer Lawson, special education supervisor

Luther Ross, general education math teacher

Paul Weiss, teacher of the hearing impaired

Pam Chang, school psychologist

John Stevens, interpreter

The meeting was held in the high school conference room after school. All participants were seated, introductions were made, and Jennifer Lawson, special education supervisor, began the meeting.

MS. LAWSON: The purpose of our meeting today is to review James's progress and to determine the services needed for the next school year. I would like to begin our meeting today by asking each person to state something positive about James. I'll begin. I have worked with James and his family since he was three, and James has matured a great deal this year. When I saw James in the hallway last week, he smiled and said hello.

MR. ROSS: I have James in my geometry class this year. I was a little apprehensive about having him in my class, but I am pleasantly surprised. James attends very well to instruction and is completing his homework. His grade to date is a B.

MR. WEISS: I have also noticed a positive change in James this year. He brings all of his work to class and is anxious to complete it before the end of the day. He is also using his planner to write assignments.

MS. CHANG: I work with James and his classmates weekly on social skills instruction, and James is always willing to role-play different situations for the class.

MR. JACKSON: James is following his curfew at home and seems to be working more on his homework.

MR. STEVENS: James does an excellent job attending to me when needed during class. He is also trying to take notes on his own.

MS. LAWSON: Thank you. We will now review James's progress in his classes and his recent assessment. Mr. Weiss, will you begin by reviewing new assessment data and describe how James is progressing?

MR. WEISS: James was recently seen for an audiological evaluation to monitor hearing levels and auditory trainer performance. As you know, an auditory trainer, or FM transmission device, helps minimize the distance and noise problems in the general education classroom. The teacher speaks into a small microphone clipped to his shirt and the student receives the sound through a desktop receiver. The audiologist used pure tone and speech reception thresholds, which revealed a bilateral moderate to severe hearing loss, poorer for the left ear. These findings were consistent with previously obtained audiograms. While James was wearing his binaural FM receiver, a significant gain in audibility was recorded. James's hearing aids were found to be in good working condition. The audiologist concluded the report by stating that the degree of James's hearing loss will continue to have an adverse effect on his communication skills and ability to achieve in the classroom without intervention. He will be monitored periodically by the audiologist and should continue to receive special services as a student with a hearing impairment. I also must say that James often doesn't wear both hearing aids. We have talked about this often, but so far this has not changed. We do consistently use the FM receiver, which helps. James, can you help us understand why you are not wearing both hearing aids?

[James looked away and shrugged his shoulders.]

MR. WEISS: This year, James has really improved in his reading ability. He is in my special class for all subjects except math and physical education. So far, he has been able to maintain average to above-average grades. He really enjoys physical education and sports. The other students admire his abilities in sports, especially soccer. In my classes, James participates when he is familiar and comfortable with the subject. Mr. Stevens, the interpreter, goes to all classes with James, and his services help in communication. James completes homework and assignments with assistance from his interpreter or me. Occasionally, he becomes agitated and sullen when working on something difficult or something he doesn't like. He doesn't often study for tests. James can produce intelligible speech when he concentrates, and he willingly corrects mispronunciations when given correct modeling. I think that sometimes James's hearing impairment makes it difficult for him to make new friends. Although he has told me he is making friends, he frequently ignores friendly gestures from his hearing peers. James may need help in making friends with his hearing peers.

MR. ROSS: James seems really motivated in math. He almost always has his work completed. Sometimes, he will ask to work with Mr. Weiss on a difficult concept, and this is fine. The interpreter also is very helpful. I will also allow him to use a calculator. I recommend that he continue in general education geometry next year.

▶▶ Questions to Ponder

▶ Whose story is this?

▶ What is my background or previous experience with the issues presented in this case?

▶ What facts are presented?

▶ What opinions are presented?

MS. LAWSON: Mr. Ross, what do you notice about James's social skills with other students?

MR. ROSS: James is really quiet and stays to himself. Other students stand around and talk before the bell rings, but James finds a seat and sits by himself.

MS. LAWSON: Mr. Jackson, how do you view James's progress so far this year?

MR. JACKSON: As far as I can tell, he's doing fine. I'm usually at work when he comes home, so he has to help out with his younger sister. He spends most of his time playing video games.

The group began to discuss specific goals for James and decided that he had made adequate progress on all of them. It was determined that James would receive the following special education services for the next school year:

- Services from the hearing impaired teacher: English, speech, social studies, science, study hall
- Related service from the interpreter: All academic classes plus physical education
- Related service from the school psychologist: a group social skills class that would meet weekly for one hour

James would continue to be integrated into general education for geometry and physical education.

The discussion then focused on the upcoming state achievement test that all tenth-grade students would be required to take during the next school year. It was explained that the test would address each student's skill level in reading, science, and mathematics. Students would have to "meet" or "exceed" standards assessed by the test to graduate from high school. This test was part of the federal "No Child Left Behind" law. First, it was decided that it was appropriate for James to take the test, even though he had a hearing impairment. The team determined that James would need specific accommodations when taking the test. They included the following:

- James will take the test in a small-group setting with the teacher of the hearing impaired.
- An interpreter for the hearing impaired will interpret any oral directions.
- The test will be administered over several sessions and days, in the afternoon.
- The interpreter will sign the math and science tests to James.
- James will be allowed to use a calculator as needed.
- Start and end times will be written on the chalkboard.
- James will use an FM receiver to adjust background noise.

James's individual education program was drafted as the group discussed each component. His father was given a copy of the completed program at the conclusion of the meeting. All participants seemed satisfied with the outcomes of the meeting.

Case Study Framework Questions

1. What makes this an exemplar case?
2. How do emotions influence behaviors in the main characters?
3. How is the factual information consistent with current professional literature?
4. Are issues oversimplified? If so, how?
5. Are people stereotyped? If so, how?
6. Discuss teacher dispositions that could facilitate interaction (i.e., self-reflection, tolerance for others, collaboration, multiple perspectives, sound ethical judgment, motivation to work with students with a variety of needs, capacity for advocacy) or that could become a barrier to working with the student discussed in the case.

Thinking Critically About the Case

1. How will each of the accommodations listed for the state test "level the playing field" for James to succeed on the test?
2. Why do you think the interpreter is not signing the reading test?
3. What skills do you think the psychologist will focus on during the weekly social skills class?

Activity

Research your state's education website and locate the type of test used to assess students at the high school level. Is the test a "high stakes" test (for example, are decisions about high school graduation dependent on the scores)? What types of accommodations are allowed for students who have disabilities? Who makes the decision about the types of accommodations used for a particular student? How is the test related to the No Child Left Behind Act?

CASE 2 "Kaleemah"

Type of Case: Exemplar

Age Level: Early Childhood

Characters

Kaleemah Smith, child with a hearing loss

Tamisha Smith, Kaleemah's mother

Jamica Brooks, early childhood teacher

Anna Konya, teacher of the hearing impaired

Brandon Lee, speech/language therapist

Everything was finally arranged. The cookies and coffee were out, the "play area" for the children and waiting area were stocked with toys for the children and magazines for the parents, and all stations for the early childhood assessments were ready. After fifteen years of organizing the annual early childhood screenings, it took considerable preparation and work! We were able to use a local church basement again this year and partition the assessment stations. I really felt that this annual screening was essential in serving young children who might have disabilities. We expected about fifty children over the next five days, and probably about nine or ten would be referred for full, comprehensive evaluations. Out of the evaluations, about five to seven children would be identified as having a disability. I was the teacher for the early childhood special education class, and children who were identified as having a disability would receive special education services from me during the next school year. The school social worker would initially meet with the parent to gather important background information, and three teachers would screen each child in the areas of concepts, motor skills, and speech and language development. A public health nurse would screen vision and hearing. My job this year, other than organizing the screening, was to meet with the parent at the end of the screening to explain the results.

At 9:00 A.M., our first student and parent entered. I greeted the parent, an African-American mother who walked hand-in-hand with her three-year-old daughter. I explained the screening process, and one of the teachers offered to walk with the child to the first station. The child, Kaleemah, was quiet, but she went with the teacher to the motor skills screening. Tamisha Smith, Kaleemah's mother, talked with the social worker.

About fifteen minutes later, Brandon Lee, our speech/language therapist, came to me with a look of concern. He told me that Kaleemah was a very pleasant, cooperative child and that she seemed interested in trying to receive the speaker's message, but that she didn't appear to be able to hear. She looked at the speaker's face and tried to repeat words, but the sounds she produced did not approximate speech. Kaleemah's words did not appear to be connected to objects or actions, and she seemed dependent on gestures.

I talked to the public health nurse, who then attempted to screen Kaleemah's hearing and vision. She was unable to be screened and could not follow directions. The other two evaluators made the same observations. Kaleemah seemed to be able to follow the evaluator when a model was given, but she was unable to follow oral requests.

▶▶ Questions to Ponder

▶ Whose story is this?

▶ What is my background or previous experience with the issues presented in this case?

▶ What facts are presented?

▶ What opinions are presented?

At the end of the screening, I knew that Kaleemah would need to be referred for a full evaluation to determine if she had a disability. I felt certain that something was interfering with her ability to speak and understand language. In talking with her mother, Tamisha, I learned that Kaleemah recently had begun attending Head Start preschool and that the teacher in that program had recommended that Tamisha bring her daughter for the screening. Tamisha was a single parent, and Kaleemah was born when her mother was seventeen years old. Tamisha lived with her mother, baby sister, two teenage aunts, a teenage uncle, step-grandmother, and grandfather. Tamisha was not employed and received services from Public Aid, Food Stamps, and Women, Infants, and Children (WIC). Tamisha was very concerned about Kaleemah's language. She said that Keleemah had tantrums when she became frustrated, which was often, and that she could not respond to requests. Kaleemah did not know any colors and occasionally used single words at home. She often took her mother's hand to show her something.

Kaleemah was able to feed herself, dress herself, and was potty trained. I told Tamisha that we suspected possible hearing difficulties, although we couldn't be certain until we further evaluated her skills. Tamisha was interested in possible early childhood programming and was willing to sign an informed consent for an in-depth evaluation.

After informed consent was signed, the IEP team met to discuss Kaleemah's screening results and to determine what additional assessments were necessary. The teacher of the hearing impaired, Anna Konya, would evaluate Kaleemah. It was also determined that Kaleemah needed a specialized evaluation of her hearing, an auditory brainstem response evaluation at the local children's hospital, and an in-depth evaluation of her speech and language skills. The evaluations were carried out over the next few weeks, and an IEP meeting was arranged to discuss the results.

Eight persons were present at the IEP meeting in which evaluations were reviewed and discussed. They included the school nurse, the teacher of the hearing impaired, the speech/language therapist, the special education supervisor, Kaleemah's mother, a social worker, a Head Start teacher, and me, the early childhood teacher. The school nurse reviewed the results from the auditory brainstem response evaluation. They indicated the presence of a moderate to severe sensorineural hearing loss in the right ear with a moderate to profound sensorineural hearing loss in the left ear. It was recommended that Kaleemah be fitted with binaural hearing aids. It was also noted that Kaleemah had a history of ear infections and tubes in her ears. Anna, the teacher of the hearing impaired, shared her observations of Kaleemah in the Head Start classroom and gave the results of a specialized evaluation. She said that Kaleemah often looked at the speaker's face and complied with gestures. She even tried to repeat words, but was unable to do so. She played cooperatively with her peers but was largely dependent on gestures to communicate. Anna stated that Kaleemah was likely to acquire intelligible speech with amplification but that she also needed to learn signs. The speech/language therapist concurred with the evaluations, stating that Kaleemah's hearing loss had hindered the development of her oral language skills. It was the consensus of the team that Kaleemah had a disability, hearing impairment, and that her disability significantly interfered with her learning.

The team then drafted Kaleemah's IEP. Her strengths were detailed first, including her ability to follow along with the group and her ability to perform age-appropriate tasks when visually shown the tasks. The adverse effects of her disability on her learning included significantly delayed oral communication skills. The following goals were drafted: developing the skills to match, count, and associate items; increasing social skills by sharing and taking turns; increasing oral expression and signing ability; improving the ability to imitate and produce oral motor movements and sounds; and improving receptive language skills. It was decided that Kaleemah would stay in the Head Start classroom during the afternoon and attend my early childhood classroom for half a day during the morning. She also required an auditory trainer in both classrooms. Kaleemah would receive direct services from the teacher of the hearing impaired (1 hour per day) and from the speech/language therapist (30 minutes per day). Both the Head Start teacher and I would consult with the teacher of the hearing impaired on a regular basis to carry out Kaleemah's goals. She would also receive initial training to learn how to use an auditory trainer in the classroom. Tamisha, Kaleemah's mother, was very pleased with the program and expressed relief at knowing that her daughter would receive intensive services.

Case Study Framework Questions

1. What makes this an exemplar case?
2. How do emotions influence behaviors in the main characters?
3. How is the factual information consistent with current professional literature?
4. Are issues oversimplified? If so, how?
5. Are people stereotyped? If so, how?
6. Discuss teacher dispositions that could facilitate interaction (i.e., self-reflection, tolerance for others, collaboration, multiple perspectives, sound ethical judgment, motivation to work with students with a variety of needs, capacity for advocacy) or that could become a barrier to working with the student discussed in the case.

Thinking Critically About the Case

1. What were the characteristics of a hearing impairment that Kaleemah displayed?
2. Why was an IEP meeting held prior to carrying out the evaluation?
3. What is an auditory trainer, and how can it be useful?
4. What types of related services would Kaleemah receive?

Activity

Contact your local school district special education office. Ask the following questions:

- When are early childhood screenings available?
- What types of assessments are used in the screenings?
- Who should be contacted if a parent thinks his or her three-year-old child has difficulty hearing?

Discuss the answers to these questions with your partner or group.

RESOURCES FOR FURTHER INVESTIGATION

Print

Luckner, J., Bowen, S., & Carter, K. (2001). Visual teaching strategies for students who are deaf or hard of hearing. *Teaching Exceptional Children, 33*(3), 38–44.

Moores, D. F. (2001). *Educating the deaf: Psychology, principles, and practices* (5th ed.). Boston: Houghton Mifflin.

Vernon, M. (2002, Summer). A half century of progress for deaf individuals. *CSD spectrum,* 12–15.

Web

Alexander Graham Bell Association for the Deaf and Hard of Hearing
http://www.agbell.org

American Society for Deaf Children
http://www.deafchildren.org

Chapter 9

Cases Involving Students with Visual Impairments

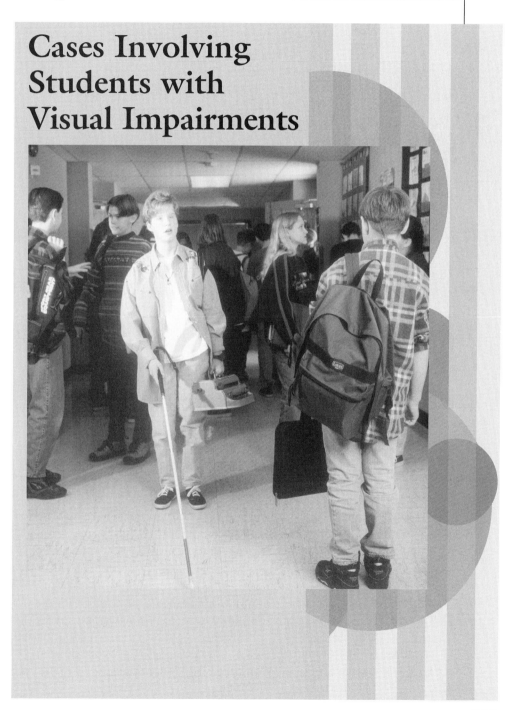

CASE 1 "Joey"

Type of Case: Contemplation

Age Level: High School

Characters

Joey Brooks, high school student with a visual impairment

Mr. Rodriguez, high school math teacher

Ms. Weiscuff, teacher of the visually impaired

Ms. Chen, special education administrator

Ms. Brooks, Joey's mother

Mr. Rodriguez, a veteran high school math teacher, felt completely puzzled about Joey, who sat in the back of his fifth-hour general math class. It was September, and Mr. Rodriguez had never taught a student who was blind before. Joey was a pleasant boy and somewhat quiet. He used a cane and was sometimes observed working with a special teacher to navigate around the building. Mr. Rodriguez had a copy of Joey's IEP, and it indicated that Joey functioned at the third-grade level in reading and math. He was to receive 1 hour of service from the itinerant teacher of the visually impaired every day. However, Mr. Rodriguez had not yet seen this teacher, and he felt at a loss as to how to help Joey. The class was beginning a review unit on multiplication. So far, Mr. Rodriguez had asked Joey to work orally while the class worked visually on worksheets.

In reviewing Joey's temporary file, Mr. Rodriquez found that Joey had been blind since birth and previously attended the residential school for the visually impaired, which was located about 2 hours away. He returned to live with his parents last year in eighth grade. After Joey was evaluated upon his return, he was labeled visually impaired and learning disabled. He was placed in an eighth-grade self-contained classroom for children who were learning disabled. For his annual review, no teachers from the high school were present. However, his eighth-grade special education teacher attended, as well as the teacher of the visually impaired and the special education supervisor. Joey was placed in general education for math and special education for other academic classes.

Mr. Rodriguez quickly made contact with the teacher of the visually impaired, Ms. Weiscuff. She gave Mr. Rodriguez some information on working with students who were blind, and she encouraged him to hold Joey accountable for schoolwork. One of the suggestions was to allow Joey to use his abacus for calculations. Ms. Weiscuff worked with Joey every day just before Mr. Rodriguez's math class. Joey also received orientation and mobility services for an hour every week to help him become more independent. The orientation and mobility instructor focused on helping Joey learn to navigate the building by himself.

However, the frustration remained. Several months went by and Mr. Rodriguez still didn't feel prepared to teach a child who was blind. Math was so visual! How could he possibly work with Joey if math was an abstract and visual subject?

> ▶▶ **Questions to Ponder**
>
> ▶ Whose story is this?
>
> ▶ What is my background or previous experience with the issues presented in this case?
>
> ▶ What facts are presented?
>
> ▶ What opinions are presented?

In November, the frustration became almost too much for Mr. Rodriguez. He was teaching a review lesson on long division. He explained to the class how to compute the answer to a problem as he worked on the board. The problem on the chalkboard was "345 divided by 20." Mr. Rodriguez said, "After you determine how many times 20 goes into 345, you write that number here (pointing). Then multiply and write that answer here (pointing). Subtract and then see how many times 20 goes into that number. If it can't go into the number, there is a remainder."

Joey sat quietly in the back of the classroom. Then Mr. Rodriguez handed out worksheets for practice and sat next to Joey to work with him individually. He talked to Joey about the concept and then asked Joey to compute one problem with the assistance of his abacus. Joey could compute basic division, but he had no idea how to compute the answer to a long division problem. The more Joey tried to show Mr. Rodriguez, the more frustrated Mr. Rodriguez felt. Finally, Joey was given a different assignment, one that involved basic division.

On another day, Joey came to class without completing his homework. When asked why, he quietly said that he had to write a report for social studies and it took him all evening to write it on his Brailler. Mr. Rodriguez told Joey that he had to complete the same work as all other students in the class and needed to organize his time more efficiently and try harder. Joey appeared to be upset but didn't say anything.

The next morning, Mr. Rodriguez contacted the special education administrator, Ms. Chen, to discuss Joey.

MR. RODRIGUEZ: Ms. Chen, I just don't know how to work with Joey! I've tried and tried to teach him math, but his visual impairment prevents him from understanding the concepts. I need help, and the teacher of the visually impaired is only here 1 hour a day. During that hour I teach a geometry class and I can't even talk to her!

MS. CHEN: Look, Mr. Rodriguez, Joey has progressed a great deal since he returned from his residential placement. The district cannot afford to hire a full-time teacher of the visually impaired for only one child. I know he can succeed. If you need help, it would be a good idea to talk to the teacher of the visually impaired.

MR. RODRIGUEZ: I am requesting an IEP team meeting to discuss Joey's progress, Ms. Chen.

MS. CHEN: I don't really think that is necessary, but I'll try to arrange one in the next week or so.

Three weeks later, Mr. Rodriguez was given a notice for an IEP meeting on Joey. Other participants included Ms. Chen, the special education administrator; Ms. Brooks, Joey's mother; and Ms. Weiscuff, the teacher of the visually impaired. The purpose of the meeting was to discuss Joey's progress and to make changes in his IEP, if appropriate. At the meeting, the participants introduced themselves and Ms. Chen stated the purpose of the meeting. She said, "Mr. Rodriguez contacted me a few weeks ago and expressed concern about Joey's progress. Mr. Rodriguez, could you tell us about how Joey is progressing in your class?"

Mr. Rodriguez clearly expressed his frustration with teaching a blind student. He said, "I have thirty other students in my class and Joey sits in the back of the classroom. I do not have enough time to individually teach Joey and I think he needs help!"

Ms. Weiscuff stated that Joey was making D's in other classes, with the exception of science, where he was failing.

Ms. Brooks said, "Joey never had this much difficulty when he was in eighth grade or when he was at the school for the visually impaired. I think he needs more special help to pass his classes. He works so hard every evening on homework, sometimes as much as four hours. He is so exhausted and is becoming somewhat depressed. It takes so much energy to complete the work assigned!"

Ultimately, the team decided that Joey needed an individual teacher's aide in all of his academic classes. The aide would work under the direction of his teacher of the visually impaired, who would train the aide to work with Joey and to communicate daily with all of Joey's teachers. Joey would also begin to work on the computer using adaptive programs. These changes were indicated on Joey's IEP. The meeting concluded.

Later that month, Ms. Chen recommended to the superintendent and board of education that an individual teacher's aide be employed to assist Joey. The recommendation was unanimously approved and an aide was hired immediately.

Mr. Rodriguez noticed a dramatic improvement with Joey. He provided the teacher of the visually impaired and aide with a long-term plan for the math curriculum and worked with the aide daily to adapt Joey's assignments. Joey was moved to the front of the room at the end of a row, and he began to participate in class by answering questions. When written work was required, the aide assisted him and retaught concepts that Joey didn't understand. At the end of the school year, Joey earned C's in all of his classes.

Case Study Framework Questions

1. What makes this a contemplation case?
2. How do emotions influence behaviors in the main characters?
3. How is the factual information consistent with current professional literature?
4. Are issues oversimplified? If so, how?
5. Are people stereotyped? If so, how?
6. Discuss teacher dispositions that could facilitate interaction (i.e., self-reflection, tolerance for others, collaboration, multiple perspectives, sound ethical judgment, motivation to work with students with a variety of needs, capacity for advocacy) or that could become a barrier to working with the student discussed in the case.

Thinking Critically About the Case

1. What could have happened at Joey's eighth-grade annual review that might have prevented the problems described?
2. How could the math teacher and the teacher of the visually impaired have collaborated?
3. During one lesson, Mr. Rodriguez worked on the chalkboard and verbally described what he was doing by saying things like, "you write that number here" and "write that answer here." How could Mr. Rodriquez have changed his language to convey understanding of the problem to Joey?
4. What other professionals should be involved, and what should they be doing?

Activity

You are a general education teacher in social studies, and you recently had a child placed in your class who is blind. With support from the teacher of the visually impaired, you have attempted the following accommodations: allowing preferential seating by the windows; requesting large-print versions of worksheets, notes, and tests; handing out class notes before the class; attempting to define words and explain concepts as you write on the board; giving extra time for assignments; and using special paper for written assignments. You meet with the teacher of the visually impaired every other week, and the student receives daily support from the teacher. Despite this assistance, you still feel that the student is not learning as well as he could. What should you, as a general education teacher, do in this situation? How will you explain your feelings to the parents? To the teacher of the visually impaired? To your special education administrator? What changes in the IEP will you suggest?

CASE 2 "Sveta"

Type of Case: Exemplar

Age Level: Elementary School

Characters

Sveta Olheno, fourth-grade student who has a visual impairment

Bill and Katerina Olheno, Sveta's parents

Mary Baker, fourth-grade teacher

Andrea Hughes, special education administrator

David Patterson, teacher of the visually impaired

Steve James, orientation and mobility instructor

Stephanie Eva, individual aide

Jarod Hauk, school social worker

Jennifer Albertson, school psychologist

I must admit that I am a little apprehensive about attending this IEP meeting. This is my fifth year as a fourth-grade teacher and I have been to many IEP meetings, but this is the first for a child who is blind. I really enjoy working with all types of children, and I know I can help them be successful. This child will be no different, I tell myself. Still, I haven't been trained in how to teach a child who is blind.

My philosophy in working with children is that all children have talents and abilities. Although some children aren't developmentally ready for fourth-grade work, all children can succeed. I don't think that all children have to learn the same things at the same time. My job is to assess each child's readiness in a skill area, plan effective lessons, and teach. I try to be respectful and fair and to use good communication skills with my students. I also help all students become independent by holding high expectations.

As I walk into the conference room, I feel confident that I can work with this child. Ms. Hughes announces that they are meeting to discuss Sveta's IEP for next year. From the introductions that follow, I gather that the teacher of the visually impaired, Mr. Patterson, worked with

Sveta last year and that Ms. Eva, the individual aide, has worked with Sveta for the past two years.

After the introductions, Ms. Hughes says, "We will begin today by discussing current assessment results on Sveta. As you know, she was recently reevaluated."

As each person reports, I write notes on a legal pad and learn many things about Sveta. I learn that she lives with both parents and three brothers, ages ten, thirteen, and fifteen. Both of her parents work as mail carriers. Sveta reached developmental milestones within normal limits until she was two years old, when she suddenly lost vision in her left eye. Several specialists diagnosed her with neurofibromatosis and optic nerve gliomas. The tumors were growing in both eyes, and Sveta had chemotherapy to reduce their size. Although she is now in remission, she lost almost all of the vision in her right eye and did not regain vision in her left eye. She only sees shadows and colors from one corner of the right eye. Sveta began receiving special education when she was three years old.

▶▶ Questions to Ponder

▶ Whose story is this?

▶ What is my background or previous experience with the issues presented in this case?

▶ What facts are presented?

▶ What opinions are presented?

The teacher for the visually impaired, Mr. Patterson, conducted a functional vision evaluation on Sveta. He says that Sveta is a delightful child, full of energy and very interested in learning. She received grades of A and B in third grade and is a quick learner. She is able to work with a light box to help her draw, color, or write, and she can identify some objects when they are placed on top of the light box. She also uses a work tray on her desk so that she can locate needed objects. She shouldn't be placed near a window because the glare interferes with her limited vision. Sveta is learning to read and write in Braille, and she recently completed the second Braille code level in reading. Sveta uses an abacus to compute addition, subtraction, and multiplication problems. She must have a Brailler, Braille paper, Brailled books and materials, adapted materials, an abacus, books on tape, Braille Lite, a Braille printer, a cane, a stand for materials, and adaptive software for the computer (JAWS for Windows).

The school psychologist, Ms. Albertson, reports that Sveta was administered the verbal portion of the *Wechsler Individual Scale of Intelligence,* third edition. She says that Sveta was very interested in the testing tasks and that she had relative strengths in general information and comprehension. Sveta's overall intelligence, prorated because of her visual impairment, was within the average range.

The orientation and mobility instructor describes his evaluation of Sveta. Although she has difficulty with mobility in unfamiliar settings, Sveta is easily able to move around the building to familiar classrooms, restrooms, and the lunchroom. She uses constant contact and is learning to walk "in step" with the cane. She is also learning to follow a route when a compass direction is verbally given to her, but she needs improvement in this area.

I am now asked how my classroom curriculum is organized. I begin telling about how children are taught in reading, math, social studies, science, and language arts. I suggest that Sveta probably will benefit from instruction that is verbal and that she probably can complete some of the written work.

Mr. Patterson, the teacher for the visually impaired, suggests that Sveta needs intensive instruction to help her learn to read Braille and to learn more about using the abacus in math. He suggests that Sveta needs special education instruction in these two areas and that she will be successful in other areas with adapted materials and a full-time aide.

I agree, and I suggest that Sveta could be assigned a "lunch buddy" and a physical education "buddy" who could walk to and from those areas with her. I state that I would like to work closely with Mr. Patterson, perhaps on a weekly basis, to discuss Sveta's progress so that she can receive the help she needs. Mr. Patterson agrees and states that he and the aide will assist Sveta in completing her written work.

The parents seem enthusiastic about Sveta's placement in my class for the majority of the day. They say that Sveta looks forward to fourth grade and that they will support her at home.

As we talk, the special education administrator, Ms. Hughes, begins to write Sveta's Individual Education Plan. As she writes something, she reads it aloud so the group has a chance to provide input. Several goals and benchmarks are specified and written in the IEP. They include the following:

Goal: Sveta will learn to read the Grade 2 Braille Code at 90 percent accuracy.

Benchmark: Sveta will complete the first half of the Grade 2 Braille Reader at 90 percent accuracy by December, to be evaluated in December by observation and test scores.

Benchmark: Sveta will complete the second half of the Grade 2 Braille Reader at 90 percent accuracy by May, to be evaluated in May by observation and test scores.

Professional Responsible: Teacher of the visually impaired.

Goal: Sveta will use the Braille Lite to complete 80 percent of her written assignments.

Benchmark: Sveta will use the Braille Lite to complete 4 of 5 language arts assignments by December, to be evaluated in May by observation.

Professional Responsible: Teacher of the visually impaired, general education teacher.

Goal: Sveta will use the abacus to complete division problems at 80 percent accuracy.

Benchmark: Sveta will divide a two-digit number by a one-digit number at 80 percent accuracy using an abacus by December, to be evaluated in December by observation.

Benchmark: Sveta will divide a three-digit number by a two-digit number at 80 percent accuracy using an abacus by May, to be evaluated in May by observation.

Professional Responsible: Teacher of the visually impaired, general education teacher.

Goal: Sveta will use her cane skills to walk "in step" 90 percent of the time.

Benchmark: Sveta will use an arc of 2 inches outside of her shoulders with a maximum of two verbal prompts 90 percent of the time, to be monitored quarterly by observation and check sheet.

Professional Responsible: Orientation and mobility instructor.

It is also suggested that Sveta needs an individual aide to assist her in the classroom and in special classes like physical education and art. Everyone agrees with this suggestion. We also decide that Sveta can take the state assessment with other children with some adaptations, including Braille tests, extended time, and individual demonstration when needed. It is determined and written in the IEP that Sveta will receive the following services:

- 50 minutes per day: services for the visually impaired in general and special education classrooms for reading and math instruction
- 360 minutes per day: individual aid in the general and special education classrooms for all subjects
- 60 minutes per week: orientation and mobility instruction in the general and special education classrooms

The special education administrator then reads the IEP to the group. After minor changes are made, she makes copies for each person. The meeting is over, and I walk with Sveta's parents to their car. I tell them that I am pleased to work with Sveta in fourth grade and that I know she will succeed. They look at me with tears in their eyes and thank me.

Although this is a challenge, I really look forward to having Sveta in my class.

Case Study Framework Questions

1. What makes this an exemplar case?
2. How do emotions influence behaviors in the main characters?
3. How is the factual information consistent with current professional literature?
4. Are issues oversimplified? If so, how?
5. Are people stereotyped? If so, how?
6. Discuss teacher dispositions that could facilitate interaction (i.e., self-reflection, tolerance for others, collaboration, multiple perspectives, sound ethical judgment, motivation to work with students with a variety of needs, capacity for advocacy) or that could become a barrier to working with the student discussed in the case.

Thinking Critically About the Case

1. How did those who attended the IEP meeting contribute to the IEP development?
2. Who are required participants in an IEP meeting? Were required participants in attendance in this IEP meeting?
3. Describe the purpose of the IEP meeting.
4. Describe the procedure used to develop Sveta's IEP.

Activity

What is your philosophy of education? How does your philosophy address using diverse skills and abilities and meeting individual needs? Write a one-page narrative describing your philosophy of education. On the basis of your written philosophy, answer the following question in writing: Should children who are blind be placed in general education classes? Why or why not? Discuss your philosophy and answer to the question with a classmate.

RESOURCES FOR FURTHER INVESTIGATION

Print

Bina, J. (1999). Schools for the visually disabled: Dinosaurs or mainstay? *Educational Leadership, 56*(6), 78–81.

Cox, P., & Dykes, M. (2001). Effective classroom adaptations for students with visual impairments. *Teaching Exceptional Children, 33*, 68–74.

Meinbach, A. M. (1999). Seeking the light: Welcoming a visually impaired student. *Middle School Journal, 31*(2), 10–17.

Spungin, S. J. (Ed.). (2001). *When you have a visually impaired student in your classroom: A guide for teachers.* New York: AFB Press.

Web

American Council of the Blind
http://www.acb.org/

American Foundation for the Blind
http://www.afb.org

Chapter 10

Cases Involving Students with Multiple and Severe Disabilities

CASE 1 "Alexandrea"

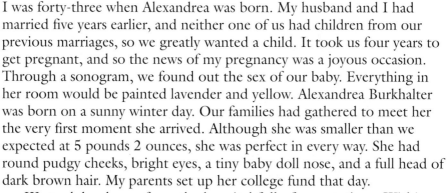

Type of Case: Exemplar

Age Level: Elementary School

Characters

Alexandrea Burkhalter, nine-year-old girl diagnosed with several disabilities

Bea Burkhalter, Alexandrea's mother

I was forty-three when Alexandrea was born. My husband and I had married five years earlier, and neither one of us had children from our previous marriages, so we greatly wanted a child. It took us four years to get pregnant, and so the news of my pregnancy was a joyous occasion. Through a sonogram, we found out the sex of our baby. Everything in her room would be painted lavender and yellow. Alexandrea Burkhalter was born on a sunny winter day. Our families had gathered to meet her the very first moment she arrived. Although she was smaller than we expected at 5 pounds 2 ounces, she was perfect in every way. She had round pudgy cheeks, bright eyes, a tiny baby doll nose, and a full head of dark brown hair. My parents set up her college fund that day.

We took her home from the hospital full of expectations. Within a week, I began to worry. Alexandrea seemed to cry most of the time. She didn't eat well and would vomit after every feeding. I went to the doctor for help. They weighed Alexandrea and found she wasn't putting on the expected weight. The doctor suggested she was colicky and that she needed to be fed smaller amounts more often. Alexandrea continued to have feeding problems. Then, she began projectile vomiting and started losing weight. At two months old, the doctors admitted Alexandrea to the hospital for tests. They found abnormally high levels of calcium in her blood, which is very unusual. The doctors also found cardiovascular abnormalities. A specialist was called in to evaluate her. The doctors decided it was best to have Alexandrea on a low-calcium diet. A special milk was prescribed. The doctors also asked to run a test, called the FISH (fluorescence in situ hybridization) test, on her blood. Four days later, Alexandrea was diagnosed with Williams syndrome.

Williams syndrome is a rare congenital disorder. The effects vary considerably. However, common characteristics include low birthweight, feeding problems, slowness in weight gain, irritability during infancy, "elfin-like" facial features, heart and blood vessel problems, dental and kidney abnormalities, sensitivity to noise, musculoskeletal problems, and intellectual disabilities.

As I looked at my beautiful daughter, her pixie-like appearance took on a different meaning. She had a disorder, which would more than likely mean a lower intellectual capacity and lifelong medical issues. My husband and I were devastated. We had waited so long for this baby, and now our joy had been turned into grief. I also felt ashamed, because I wondered if we should have even tried to have children. Alexandrea would probably never use her college fund for higher education. My dreams had vanished. I thought about the future and wondered if I would send her off to kindergarten happy to learn. Would we ever videotape her winning a school spelling bee, help her buy a dress for the prom, send her to college, or cry at her wedding?

▶▶ Questions to Ponder

▶ Whose story is this?

▶ What is my background or previous experience with the issues presented in this case?

▶ What facts are presented?

▶ What opinions are presented?

Alexandrea is nine now. She has made a tremendous amount of progress since her birth. Her feeding problems were extreme during the first year of her life, but they have lessened considerably. Although many children with Williams syndrome have mild cardiovascular problems, Alexandrea has had chronic heart problems, and she is facing open-heart surgery. She also had chronic urinary tract infections and persistent bedwetting. Alexandrea was slow to reach all of her developmental milestones; she began talking when she was four.

Fortunately, Alexandrea received special services even before she was a year old. The doctors helped us seek out in-home physical therapy and special education services as soon as Alexandrea was diagnosed with the disability. These services were free. When Alexandrea was three, she began going to a preschool for children with special needs in our school district.

She was diagnosed with a moderate cognitive impairment in kindergarten, and she was placed in a self-contained special education classroom. She loves school, loves her teachers, and has a very outgoing personality. She is extremely impulsive, moves constantly, and has difficulty maintaining concentration. Alexandrea was diagnosed with attention deficit hyperactivity disorder when she was seven. She also has difficulty with anxiety and was diagnosed with generalized anxiety disorder three months ago. She is fearful of being alone, refuses to sleep in her own room, and needs a consistent routine. If her routine is disrupted, she cries excessively, pulls her hair, screams, and shakes as though she is freezing. Medication has helped with both her attentional problems and anxiety.

I have to admit, I wonder what our life would be like if Alexandrea had been born without Williams syndrome. What would she have looked like? Could I have been the one going to museums and the movies with my child? My friends complain about the arguments they have with their children over homework and their children's disrespectful language. I wish Alexandrea had the skills to "talk back"; instead she tantrums.

I am seeing a counselor, who told me my feelings were similar to feelings of grief. She explained that whenever there's a loss of hopes and dreams, whenever you confront the reality that "something is different, something is wrong" with your child, you experience grief. Feelings of shock, guilt, anger, depression, blame, and denial are common. But this kind of grief is not finite, like grief from the death of a child. It comes from experiences that continually fall short of your expectations. The therapist called it "nonfinite" grief.

Both the grief and the daily tasks of dealing with Alexandrea's disability have put a lot of stress on my marriage. The constant medical issues, countless doctor's appointments, home visits by early childhood specialists, school evaluations, testing, IEP meetings, and outside therapy have put a strain on my family emotionally and financially. My husband seems to look at me as the expert and isn't involved with Alexandrea's services. He says I'm overly involved and wishes I had more time to enjoy the things we used to do together. We have started seeing the counselor together, and things seem to be getting better between us. We are learning to share the responsibility for Alexandrea and to share our grief. We seem to have both lost a lot to this disability and gained a lot from this child.

We now see this disability as just another way that children differ from each other. Children with disabilities are children first: they need to love and be loved, and they hold the promise of future gifts to share. No matter what the future brings for Alexandrea, we will be there for her as long as we can. We hope she will be able to live independently or semi-independently, continue to enjoy music, and lead a full and happy life.

Case Study Framework Questions

1. What makes this an exemplar case?
2. How do emotions influence behaviors in the main characters?
3. How is the factual information consistent with current professional literature?
4. Are issues oversimplified? If so, how?
5. Are people stereotyped? If so, how?
6. Discuss teacher dispositions that could facilitate interaction (i.e., self-reflection, tolerance for others, collaboration, multiple perspectives, sound ethical judgment, motivation to work with students with a variety of needs, capacity for advocacy) or that could become a barrier to working with the student discussed in the case.

Thinking Critically About the Case

1. Federal law ensures services to children with disabilities and their families from birth to age twenty-one. When did Alexandrea begin receiving services, and what system helped to establish those services?
2. What is a congenital disorder?
3. What characteristics of Williams syndrome does Alexandrea exhibit?
4. Why would Alexandrea's disability be considered a multiple disability?
5. What is nonfinite grief, and how did it affect Bea Burkhalter and her family?

Activity

Guided Conversation: Break into pairs and discuss the following questions. Deal with one question at a time, and allow each person to respond fully to each question. Remember to keep the answers confidential. If you wish to share information with the class, please share only your information, not your partner's. If you do not feel comfortable answering any question, you can pass.

- I experienced a personal loss when . . .
- The feelings of grief I experienced were . . .
- My grief was similar to the grief described in this case when . . .
- Something I learned from this case is . . .
- As a professional, I can help parents of children with disabilities in the grief process by . . .

CASE 2 "Tyvon"

Type of Case: Contemplation

Age Level: Middle School

Characters

Tyvon Jones, eighth-grade student with a cognitive disability and cerebral palsy

Tyrell Jones, eighth-grade student and Tyvon's twin brother

Marcus Jones, Tyvon and Tyrell's older brother

Mr. and Mrs. Jones, Tyvon and Tyrell's parents

Sara Wilson, eighth-grade special education teacher at Eastgate Middle School

Kisha Morgan, ninth-grade special education teacher at James Rogers High School

Regina Martin, ninth-grade history teacher at James Rogers High School

Dr. Robert Jackson, principal at James Rogers High School

Kay Webber, school psychologist at James Rogers High School

Regina Martin glanced at the clock on the wall. It was 3:15 P.M., only fifteen more minutes. She couldn't believe her luck! Of all the ninth-grade teachers, why had she been selected to attend this IEP meeting? It's not that she had anything against students with disabilities, but this matter really wasn't any of her concern. This student would probably never see the inside of a general education history class, so why was it so important for her to be the "representative for general education"? She just couldn't understand. After all, she would probably never even see this boy. Everyone knew that James Rogers High School wasn't equipped to deal with mentally retarded kids. Those kinds of kids always remained at the middle school, where the facilities were newer and they had trained teachers to deal with them.

From what she understood about Tyvon Jones, he had cerebral palsy, used a wheelchair, and couldn't speak understandably. He probably had a low IQ as well. Regina had one of Tyvon's older brothers in her history class several years ago. She remembered him mentioning that he had younger twin brothers, one of whom had sustained birth trauma and was disabled. The other, he said, had average ability. Yes, Regina remembered Marcus Jones. He was a charismatic and athletic ninth-grader. He was an average student, but Regina assumed he could do much better if he applied himself. He had since graduated and gone on to a state university to play football. Even though Regina had Marcus in her class several years ago, she didn't really know his family and felt that attending this IEP was a waste of her time. She had enough to do with the state testing, lesson plans, and working with students with special needs who *would* actually be in her classes. After all, Dr. Jackson would be in attendance. He would certainly be able to sign the papers and fulfill the "legal requirement." Why should this IEP or this student be any different?

> ## ▶▶ Questions to Ponder
>
> ▶ Whose story is this?
>
> ▶ What is my background or previous experience with the issues presented in this case?
>
> ▶ What facts are presented?
>
> ▶ What opinions are presented?

Mr. and Mrs. Jones walked down the familiar halls of James Rogers High School. They knew that they were in for a battle. But after raising five boys they had learned to pick their battles, and this one was worth it. For the most part they always had good relations with the school administrators and teachers. In their opinion, this situation was just not acceptable. In fact, it was downright unfair. That was part of the reason they requested that Ms. Regina Martin be in attendance at this IEP. Their older son, Marcus, had had Ms. Martin for ninth-grade history, and he spoke about her lessons on civil rights and discrimination so often they knew she would notice when an injustice was occurring. Marcus told them how Ms. Martin had discussed how to be aware of discrimination and how they should fight for justice whenever possible. Each one of their three older boys had attended James Rogers High School, and if they had anything to do with it, the two younger ones would also.

Each one of their boys seemed to be athletically gifted, all except Tyvon. They watched in the stands and stadium each year, with Tyvon right there next to them waving his James Rogers Eagles banner faster than anyone else, as each of the older boys excelled in either basketball or football. Now it looked as if Tyrell would be the next football star in their family. At 5 feet 10 inches and 180 pounds, he was a first-string tailback in middle school and was looking forward to being a varsity player. Tyvon, on the other hand, had been in a wheelchair all of his life. However, he was the biggest James Rogers High School Eagles fan around. He seemed to sparkle every time he watched one of his brothers on the court or field. Why would the administration deny him the right to attend school at James Rogers High?

They knew that the program for students with mental retardation was housed at the middle school. They knew that all of the other children with moderate to severe cognitive disabilities would stay at Eastgate Middle School through the age of twenty-one. But they also knew that the law said students have the right to a least restrictive environment. How could Tyvon even interact with his "peers" if they had all moved on to the high school? How could the district make Tyrell leave his brother behind? It wasn't that they wanted him included in general education classes. They knew he needed life skills instruction and transition/vocational skills training. However, they did want him to be a freshman at James Rogers High just like the rest of his brothers.

Regina Martin walked into a room that was stifled with tension. She smiled weakly at Mr. and Mrs. Jones. Mr. Jones rose to shake her hand.

"It's nice to see you again, Ms. Martin," he said.

"Thank you," she replied. "How is Marcus?"

"He is in his first semester at State and playing football, as usual. We think he is working hard and staying out of trouble," he laughed.

Kay Webber, the school psychologist, asked everyone to have a seat so the meeting could begin. The small room was filled to capacity with school faculty. Regina noticed that the Joneses seemed to look bewildered, and she felt for them. It must be difficult raising a child with a disability. It also seemed that everyone in the room looked so official. The principal and school psychologist were wearing suits. The teachers were all holding files that were at least 2 inches thick. How long would this meeting take? It didn't seem to be the "run of the mill" IEP that she was used to attending for students with learning disabilities or emotional/behavior disorders who needed accommodations in history class. This looked big, and she wondered why. After a brief introduction, Sara Wilson, the eighth-grade special education teacher at Eastgate, began to describe Tyvon. She described Tyvon as having spastic diplegic cerebral palsy, which necessitated the use of a wheelchair. His language was also affected by his cerebral palsy, and he used some assistive technology to help with his communication. He was also diagnosed with moderate mental retardation. Regina was struck with the negativity in the terminology and phrases. Sara Wilson and Kisha Morgan took turns telling the Joneses what their child couldn't do and what they could do to address his weaknesses. It seemed to go on forever. Finally, Kay Webber took the floor again. She stated that the recommendation of the team was for Tyvon to continue his placement in the program at Eastgate Middle School for students with mental retardation. The teachers, Sara Wilson and Kisha Morgan, would be able to address his physical, communication, academic, and transition needs. He would be given life skills and community living training. Regina listened to the school psychologist describe the program. It sounded reasonable. It even sounded good. Tyvon would get all of his needs met, and he wouldn't have to adapt to a new environment. What could be wrong with that?

Finally, Mr. and Mrs. Jones were given a chance to speak. Regina noticed that Mrs. Jones's voice cracked as she began. "I don't feel that this is Tyvon's least restrictive environment," she said.

"What makes you say that?" countered Kay Webber.

"You don't know Tyvon the way we know him. All he ever does is talk about the James Rogers High School Eagles. His older brother's girlfriend painted the mascot on his bedroom wall. He goes to every home game his brothers are in. His dream is to be an Eagle. Doesn't *least restrictive environment* mean educated and socialized with nondisabled peers? Well, if Tyvon is in another building, how could he be either? We want him to have the chance to go to school pep rallies and be a part of the school community. He talks about going to high school with his brother Tyrell all the time. We tried to explain to him that he would stay at Eastgate, but his answer was, 'why?' So we want to know why!"

Dr. Jackson, the high school principal, tried to explain that James Rogers High didn't have the kind of facilities Tyvon needed and the teachers and therapists were all housed at the middle school. He talked about the building structure, the lack of air conditioning in the older parts of the building, and the need for repairs to many rooms. He also talked about a proposed boundary shift and possible overcrowding. Regina looked at the tears in Mrs. Jones's eyes. She found out that there were only seven students in the program for students with multiple disabilities in grades 9–12 for next year. She knew that James Rogers was renovating several rooms and that enrollments had dropped. All she could think was, Tyvon wants to know why. She hadn't even considered his feelings. She thought that kids with cognitive disabilities were just happy to do what they were told. Should he have a choice? Why was the program for students with significant disabilities in grades 9–12 at the middle school?

Case Study Framework Questions

1. What makes this a contemplation case?
2. How do emotions influence behaviors in the main characters?
3. How is the factual information consistent with current professional literature?
4. Are issues oversimplified? If so, how?
5. Are people stereotyped? If so, how?
6. Discuss teacher dispositions that could facilitate interaction (i.e., self-reflection, tolerance for others, collaboration, multiple perspectives, sound ethical judgment, motivation to work with students with a variety of needs, capacity for advocacy) or that could become a barrier to working with the student discussed in the case.

Thinking Critically About the Case

1. What is a "least restrictive environment," and how does it apply to this case?
2. What are spastic diplegic cerebral palsy and moderate mental retardation?
3. List the reasons Mr. and Mrs. Jones wanted Tyvon to attend James Rogers High School.
4. Why did Mr. and Mrs. Jones request that Regina Martin attend the IEP?
5. Did Regina Martin's view change during the case?

Activity

Put an X on the scale below indicating your belief about the issue presented in this case.

1	2	3	4	5

Tyvon should remain at Eastgate MS   Tyvon should go to James Rogers HS

Divide into groups of those who indicated 1s, 2s, 3s, 4s, and 5s. Discuss your common beliefs. Then divide the groups again, mixing the groups so that those with different opinions are in each group. Debate the different viewpoints. After the debate, write a 1-minute reflection on dispositions seen during the debate.

RESOURCES FOR FURTHER INVESTIGATION

Print

Agran, M., Alper, S., & Wehmeyer, M. (2002). Access to the general curriculum for students with significant disabilities: What it means to teachers. *Education and Training in Mental Retardation and Developmental Disabilities, 37*(2), 123–133.

Denham, A., & Lahm, E. A. (2001). Using technology to construct alternate portfolios of students with moderate and severe disabilities. *Teaching Exceptional Children, 33*(5), 10–17.

Friend, M., & Bursuck, W. (2002). *Including students with special needs: A practical guide for classroom teachers.* Boston: Allyn and Bacon.

Grigal, M., Neubert, D. A., & Moon, M. (2002). Postsecondary options for students with significant disabilities. *Teaching Exceptional Children, 35*(2), 68–73.

Kennedy, C. (2004). *Including students with severe disabilities.* Boston: Allyn and Bacon.

Parsons, M. B., & Reid, D. (1999). Training basic teaching skills to paraeducators of students with severe disabilities: A one-day program. *Teaching Exceptional Children, 31*(4), 48–54.

Ruef, M. B., & Turnbull, A. P. (2002). The perspectives of individuals with cognitive disabilities and/or autism on their lives and their problem behavior. *Journal of the Association for Persons with Severe Handicaps, 27*(2), 125–140.

Tyler, J. S., & Colson, S. (1994). Common pediatric disabilities: Medical aspects and educational implications. *Focus on Exceptional Children, 27*(4), 1–16.

Wolf, P. S., & Hall, T. E. (2003). Making inclusion a reality for students with severe disabilities. *Teaching Exceptional Children, 35*(4), 56–61.

Web

Cerebral Palsy: A Guide for Care
http://gait.aidi.udel.edu/res695/homepage/pd_ortho/clinics/c_palsy/cpweb.htm

Williams Syndrome Association
http://www.williams-syndrome.org

Council for Exceptional Children
http://www.cec.sped.org

Chapter 11

Cases Involving Students with Physical Disabilities and Health Impairments

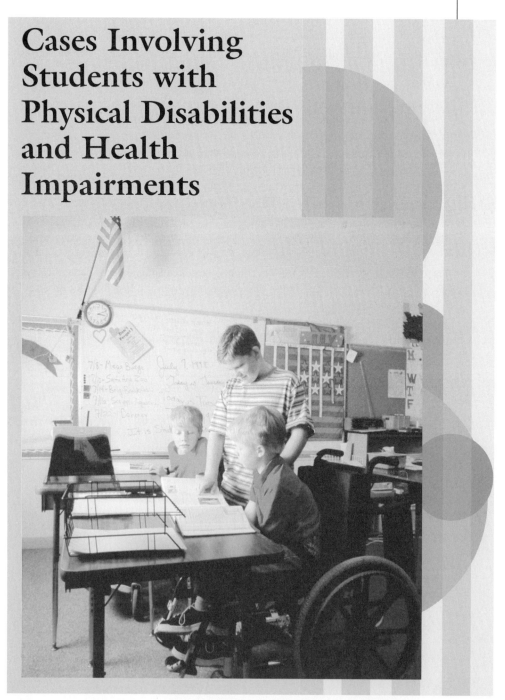

CASE 1 "Mark"

Type of Case: Exemplar

Age Level: Elementary School

Characters

Mark Lynn, second-grade child with Duchenne muscular dystrophy

Patty Lynn, Mark's mother

Pam Chang, special education teacher

Barbara O'Donnell, second-grade teacher

Tom Champion, principal

Brenda Higgins, occupational therapist

Robin Hinkley, physical therapist

The IEP meeting was held in the second-grade classroom around a small round table. Mark's special education teacher, Ms.Chang, led the meeting.

Ms. Chang began by saying, "The purpose of the meeting today is to review Mark's IEP and determine if there is a need for more intensive services." Then all present introduced themselves and stated their relation to Mark and how they wanted to be addressed. Then Ms. Chang turned to Ms. Lynn.

Ms. CHANG: Patty, I spoke with you last week when we were setting up this meeting. I explained to you at that time that we would be talking about how Mark has done this year and would be discussing his need for more intensive services for the remainder of this year. I told you that we would be looking at his current performance and making decisions as to the intensity of services needed.

Ms. LYNN: Thank you for calling. Your call gave me a chance to think about the changes we will discuss today. Sometimes I still feel upset about Mark's disease, and this gave me time to think clearly about possible changes without becoming emotional.

Ms. CHANG: Thanks, Patty. We try to encourage parents to participate in IEP meetings without fear that they are going to be surprised by something we may say. I would like to begin the meeting by going around the room and asking each of you to tell the group about some of Mark's strengths or abilities. I'll start. Mark is a very happy boy. He is friendly and loves to be around people.

DR. CHAMPION: I see Mark in the cafeteria and in the halls. He always has a grin on his face and seems happy and content.

MS. O'DONNELL: Academically, Mark is progressing very well. He reads above average when compared to other children and excels in math. He also has many friends, all of whom want to help him when needed.

MS. LYNN: Overall, Mark feels well. He has not been in the hospital once this year! When he initially began taking prednisone, he seemed stronger. However, lately he has been stumbling frequently. He still looks forward to school every day.

MS. HIGGINS: Mark is able to feed himself, and he asks for help when needed. He is still able to write his assignments.

MS. HINKLEY: Mark is fun to work with. He is walking with assistance. He sits in a regular chair and has been able to maintain motion in his joints, which has prevented contractures, or fixation of the joints.

MS. CHANG: Thank you. I would like everyone to turn to page 3 of Mark's current IEP. We are going to review his progress on the goals and objectives and discuss those that need to be addressed in the summer.

The IEP team reviewed the goals delineating what Mark could do relative to what the expectation was when the IEP was written. The "can do" information was written on the new IEP under "current level of performance." After the goals were reviewed, it was apparent that Mark had regressed physically. The discussion continued.

MS. CHANG: Patty, can you help us understand how Mark is progressing physically?

MS. LYNN: Yes. As you know, Mark has done well for a child with Duchenne muscular dystrophy. He's now seven and has been able to function independently for the most part. We use his wheelchair only when we walk long distances, like at the shopping mall. Ms. O'Donnell has been great to help him when needed. However, Ms. O'Donnell and I talked recently, and Mark is becoming weaker. Since he began taking prednisone, he has gained so much weight and his muscles are weaker, so it is harder for him to get around by himself.

MS. O'DONNELL: Yes, Patty and I have recently talked about Mark's growing muscle weakness. At the beginning of the year, Mark was able to walk by himself around the building and sit in a regular desk.

Because he has gained so much weight and has continuing muscle weakness, I feel that I need to be with him as he walks around the building. One day, he fell in the hallway, and I wasn't sure I could help him up. I'm really worried that I won't be there if he falls or that one of his friends won't be able to pick him up.

Ms. Hinkley: Mark is at the age with Duchenne muscular dystrophy when his muscles become much weaker. Even though the prednisone helps, a side effect is significant weight gain. Although Mark needs to maintain strengthening exercises and independence, he may need to think about using a wheelchair for at least part of the day.

▶▶ Questions to Ponder

▶ Whose story is this?

▶ What is my background or previous experience with the issues presented in this case?

▶ What facts are presented?

▶ What opinions are presented?

Ms. O'Donnell: I really think we need to think about more help for Mark physically. With his weight gain, I am not able to lift him if he falls or to assist him in the restroom. I want to maintain his independence, but his safety is important.

Ms. Hinkley: I wonder if it might be possible for you, Patty, to send Mark's folding wheelchair with him to school, so that he could use it in the hallways. I also wonder if Mark might need an assistant with him when he moves around the building and in the restroom. I could train both Ms. O'Donnell and the assistant to use a transfer board to move him in and out of his wheelchair. I will, of course, continue to work with Mark to maximize motion in his joints.

Ms. Lynn: I have been thinking about my goals for Mark. Although I want him to remain as independent as possible, I would feel so relieved if Mark had the extra assistance. We could easily transport his wheelchair to and from school. His doctor said that he could use it when necessary. I really think he is at a point where he needs to use the wheelchair. It would also be very helpful to have an assistant with him at certain times.

The team planned Mark's services and planned to place a half-time assistant with Mark beginning the next week. At the end of the meeting, Mark's IEP was completed and Ms. Lynn said, "I appreciate your willingness to consider Mark's changing needs."

Case Study Framework Questions

1. What makes this an exemplar case?
2. How do emotions influence behaviors in the main characters?
3. How is the factual information consistent with current professional literature?
4. Are issues oversimplified? If so, how?
5. Are people stereotyped? If so, how?
6. Discuss teacher dispositions that could facilitate interaction (i.e., self-reflection, tolerance for others, collaboration, multiple perspectives, sound ethical judgment, motivation to work with students with a variety of needs, capacity for advocacy) or that could become a barrier to working with the student discussed in the case.

Thinking Critically About the Case

1. To what extent was the parent involved in the decisions made at the IEP meeting?
2. Did the IEP team make appropriate decisions about Mark's special services? Why or why not?
3. How did the IEP team focus on Mark's strengths?
4. What other professionals should be involved, and what should they be doing?

Activity

Conduct a web search on the disability *muscular dystrophy*. What are the characteristics of Duchenne muscular dystrophy?

CASE 2 "Kate"

Type of Case: **Exemplar and Contemplation**

Age Level: **Kindergarten**

Characters

> *Kate,* child in kindergarten with physical and health disabilities
>
> *Mrs. Rita Gonzales,* kindergarten teacher
>
> *Mrs. Nancy Williams,* individual aide

Kate was a normally developing child until the age of one year, when she developed bacterial meningitis. She stayed in the hospital for five months, where she had one leg and one arm amputated, along with significant loss of facial tissue. She required a tracheotomy for one year after the hospitalization. Because of the illness, Kate had numerous surgeries, including reconstructive surgery on her face. Kate was tube-fed for eight months after her return home from the hospital. About six months after her return home, she was fitted with prostheses for her leg and arm. By the time Kate was three years old, she exhibited significant delays in language, cognitive skills, and motor skills. She was placed for two years in a full-day early childhood program where she received intensive occupational therapy (OT), physical therapy (PT), and speech and language therapy.

After two years in the early childhood program, Kate made considerable progress. According to Kate's physical and occupational therapists, she was able to maneuver herself by motorized wheelchair throughout the school with the assistance of an aide for safety and direction. The wheelchair was turned off in the classroom to allow Kate to fully participate with the class and to avoid distraction. Kate used shoulder straps when she was in the wheelchair. She also required total assistance for transfers from the wheelchair to the floor or toilet. She was able to sit on the floor with assistance and could crawl independently. In the bathroom, Kate required assistance in sitting on the toilet for safety. She used a right arm prosthesis and a left leg prosthesis, but she was unable to put weight on her legs for an extended period of time. She wore the prostheses intermittently throughout the day.

Upon entering general education kindergarten, Kate exhibited some strengths, including the ability to eat and drink independently. She needed improvement in several skills, such as moving through congested areas in the building, retrieving small items from the floor, cutting and applying tape, inserting paper into a folder, removing a jar lid, drinking from a water fountain, organizing written items, and locating three keys to carry out computer functions. She functioned within the mild mental impairment range in cognitive skills. The IEP team determined that Kate would benefit from full integration in the general education kindergarten program, with a full-time individual aide. She would be taught to use her artificial arm for control of a paper or book and would learn to use Alpha Smart for writing and spelling.

Kate's individual aide, Nancy Williams, was employed and trained to meet her daily needs. Kate was placed in a kindergarten classroom with twenty children beginning in August. The kindergarten teacher, Mrs. Rita Gonzales, was a second-year teacher and was willing to work with Kate. Mrs. Gonzales and Nancy, in consultation with Kate's therapists and special education teacher, worked for several days prior to the beginning of the school year to plan for Kate. Kate's family was very involved in her education and fully supportive of the program, although her mother expressed concern for Kate's safety.

▶▶ Questions to Ponder

▶ Whose story is this?

▶ What is my background or previous experience with the issues presented in this case?

▶ What facts are presented?

▶ What opinions are presented?

It was decided that Nancy would write brief notes daily about Kate's progress so that the IEP team and her family could review her program frequently and make any necessary program adjustments. The following selected samples were taken from the daily records that were kept on Kate's progress throughout the year. The daily input was brief, highlighting a few points that stood out in her days. The samples cover the time period between August 18 and May 25.

DAILY LOG

August
___

August 18: First day of school. Kate seemed to enjoy everything about school. The excited children only added to Kate's excitement. She followed quite well throughout the day. The activities were fast-paced and fun. One project involved coloring. The children had to finish the coloring project before going on to free play. Kate wanted to play and not "work." She colored a little, said she was done, and pushed the paper away. I told her it had to be done before free play. She purposely dropped the crayon on the floor. I said I would just wait until she was ready to finish, and we sat a few minutes. When she saw the other children playing after their project was completed, she decided to finish hers. She needed encouragement from the teacher to keep going before she finished coloring the picture. The rest of the day went well. She lay quietly during rest time, which I know she doesn't usually enjoy. She struggles to push herself in her wheelchair down the hallways and needs considerable encouragement.

August 24: When the teacher is working with the class, Kate likes to play with things that are on the table instead of watching what the teacher is doing and saying. When given a coloring project, she said, "I don't wanna" and pushed her paper out of the way. Today she wanted to push her wheelchair in the hallway. She seems motivated to independently maneuver her wheelchair to outdoor recess because she knows there is a friend waiting for her. The children are very warm toward Kate, and she really enjoys all the attention. Kate questions everyone about who their teacher is, where they live, etc. After recess, it was back to work. She didn't want to finish writing her name; she said "I can't" and played with the little booklet they were supposed to color and tore the front page. At that point we stopped, and I sent the booklet home.

August 26: Kate is willing to maneuver herself a little more in the hallways (with encouragement). However, if anyone walks by, especially rows of children, she will stop and watch until everyone is out of view. She takes in all of this kind of activity and seems to have trouble concentrating on other activities in the classroom. In the classroom during classtime, she pulls out her supplies, folder, etc. while the teacher is teaching. I know she is hearing some of what is said because she talks about it later, but she misses what is on the board or anything the teacher is holding. When she tries to get objects out of her desk, I will cover it with my hand. She doesn't like this and tries to pull my hand away.

    An interesting thing happened today. The children's' nametags have their personal identification number (PIN) and their bus number listed. Kate's nametag is in her folder because she prefers not to wear it. In the lunchroom, I told her the

(continued)

PIN to tell the cashier, and I helped her find the numbers on the keypad. Later in the classroom, the teacher asked the children to write their bus number on a little bus they made. When I asked Kate what bus she rode, she gave me her exact PIN! She remembered the PIN even though we didn't practice it. Even though the teacher was looking for the bus number, I thought it was significant that Kate remembered the three-digit PIN.

Toileting is more scheduled this year to try to keep her in the classroom as much as possible. We go about every hour, or more often if necessary. In the bathroom, we practice singing or other things that the teacher has talked about. Kate sang about half the months of the year! She is dry about half the time, but she hasn't gone on the toilet yet. I ask her throughout the day if she needs to use the restroom, and I remind her to tell me if she does. About half an hour before afternoon bus, she was working at her desk and stopped and stared at me, twice. I asked her what was wrong and she said "nothing" both times. I think she knew she was having a bowel movement because not long afterward I realized she had. I asked her about it, but she said she didn't know what I was talking about.

August 29: The class was working on coloring pictures of a body that took up about two and a half sheets of paper. This is quite a bit of coloring, and usually Kate gets tired of working. I was prepared to let her stop before she was finished. She surprised me and colored it quickly with little encouragement. She really likes to play with any object within reach while the teacher is teaching. I like to leave the table the way the other children have theirs, but I usually have to move her things out of the way before the end of the day, or sometimes I pull her chair away from the table. Kate was very cooperative today, which she must have realized, because she said, "I'm not being mad today." The class played Bingo. She played most of one game (with encouragement), but as the class played a couple more games, she preferred to play with the pieces and turned her paper over.

August 30: The children were writing their names today. Kate said, "I don't wanna" and threw her pencil on the floor. She can make most of the letters in her name, so I'm not sure why she refused. I'm guessing it may just be a little over-whelming when she sees the other children finish and play. At times, the playtime is an incentive for her to get her work completed, and at other times she just quits. At first, the teacher and I were going to have her finish her work during free play, but she was missing too much social time. It's her favorite time. Now we're going to just have her quit after she tries for a period of time. When the class recites (alphabet, numbers, etc.), Kate sometimes moves her lips along, but usually she will just watch everyone else say it. Today we realized that Kate's wooden chair might need some sort of upper body restraint because a lap belt won't keep her safely on the chair. As she sat in her wooden chair with the belt on, I pulled her about a foot away from her table because she was trying to get her folder out again. But this time, as she reached, she lost balance and started to fall forward. I was standing right by her, and she fell against me. The teacher and I both had our hands on her right away. We plan to talk to Kate's therapist about the chair. In the meantime, we will make an arm harness that will attach through an opening in the back of the chair.

September

September 16: The class went apple picking this morning. I carried Kate in the orchard instead of using the wheelchair so she could reach the apples better. She really enjoyed the whole trip. There were no socks for Kate's legs, so I couldn't put her leg on today. Later, Kate had physical and occupational therapy. It was a busy day!

September 20: Kate did well with her wheelchair in the hall again. Sometimes she will turn around and purposely go the other way to wheel into the wall and act like she's stuck. She got her name on the board for pinching me today. We feel that she does know what's expected and that it's important that she understand there are consequences for inappropriate behavior.

September 26: Kate didn't have her prosthetic leg this week. A toilet seat frame was installed in the bathroom that holds a removable high back with a chest harness and a buckle. It helps Kate sit more safely and comfortably. The straps do hold her more securely, although it is a balancing act to get her in the frame with her artificial arm. Time does not permit taking the arm off every time we use the bathroom. When she is wearing her leg, it comes off whenever she uses the bathroom.

Kate did OK in the hall. She still takes her time, but she can keep a steady pace as long as she is receiving encouragement. This afternoon, though, she said, "YOU push!" She wouldn't budge. So I just told her where I would meet her, and I walked down the hall and didn't look back. I waited around the corner and watched her to be sure none of the children would push her along. Eventually, she maneuvered herself down the hallway to meet me.

We played color/shape bingo today. Kate got through about three-quarters of the game and then took the markers off and started stacking them.

She played with her number paper and drew zigzags across the paper instead of tracing the zeros. The teacher took the paper away and gave her a different one. It went a little better with encouragement.

Kate did well in the hall. Occasionally she still goes the other way, and I know it's just a game for her. After we're finished in the bathroom, I usually secure her

(continued)

in the wheelchair and tell her to meet me in class. Then I clean up the bathroom and meet her in the hall. Twice, she purposely went the other way and ended up playing in the water fountain. I told her she would get her name pulled if it happened again. The next time she was supposed to be headed back to class, she went the opposite direction and was playing in the water again. She did get her name pulled. When I put her on the bus that afternoon, she said, "I don't want my name pulled!"

October

October 11: Mornings usually go well. Kate wrote her name, but she stubbornly refused to write in her journal. After a couple of "sit and wait" periods, she told me she was ready and wrote in her journal. I held her wrist to guide her hand, and she made the letters quite well.

Kate enjoyed the firehouse field trip. However, before we left, she talked about being afraid that something would scare her. We talked at length about what she would see at the firehouse. Overall, she did just fine and participated in all of the activities. She tolerated her leg very well. Because of the field trip I didn't put her leg on until 10:45, and she didn't ask to have it off until 2:00. She had PT and OT during that time, too. She also glued pieces of paper together to make a fire truck along with the class.

May

May 21: The class is having end-of-the-year testing. They started with name writing. Kate needed encouragement to keep going. Right after writing names, there was a number-writing test. Kate wrote the numbers 0 to 10. The numbers were not all clear, but as I watched her write them, I could see that she had the right idea. Some of the letters were very recognizable. I had to stay with her to keep her on task and remind her to stay inside the squares. When she got stuck, the only help I offered her was to have her start counting from the beginning to figure it out. The next test was a cutting test. She cut with me only holding the paper. The shape was a star, so there were only straight lines.

The best excitement of the day was a baby ground hog that the teacher brought in. The children loved watching it drink from a bottle.

Kate did well with practicing starting and stopping with the wheelchair today. She didn't have to start over.

The class wrote in their journals today. Kate did well again. She was typing the words almost as fast as I wrote them. If she got aggravated because of making a mistake, she seemed to lose her confidence and make more mistakes. All in all, she did very well on her sentence, with only a few errors. Stories were read in the afternoon; "Jack and the Beanstalk" was one of them. The children each made a picture of themselves climbing the beanstalk. The pictures were displayed on a tall beanstalk in the hallway.

May 23: The class are not having learning centers anymore, where they individually rotate from one learning station to another. They started the day as a large group with their calendars. Kate's calendar wasn't with her today, so we talked about the day and date.

    The teacher had given each child a farm coloring book and crayons that were donated by the ladies from the Farm Bureau. They read and discussed each page.

    Testing has been going on all week. Kate did the tests along with the class this morning, and we tried to make up tests from the days she was absent throughout the day. We didn't try to get her to finish, because there was quite a bit of catch-up work. Kate did seem tired and slow during the testing. I had to encourage her and repeat directions continually during the work. I could tell she wasn't doing her best work. I'm sure she wasn't quite up to it.

    The class had a visit from a preschool class today. The children love to show them the classroom. Kate knew several children in this group.

    Kate had speech this morning, and she did well. I gave her several M & M's for her good work. The afternoon was spent on silent reading, extra playtime, watching the baby ground hog, and listening to stories read by the teacher.

May 25: Kate steered well with her electric wheelchair today. She followed along with her calendar accurately and quickly.

    I took her to a quiet room to finish her testing. Yesterday she was very distractible. She stayed with the work most of the time this morning. I did have to repeat directions frequently. She preferred to talk about other things.

    The class listened to stories about farming. I didn't have Kate practice stopping her wheelchair today. There were so many end-of-the-year fun projects going on that I didn't want her to miss. It was the class's last music class of the year today. They will all miss the music teacher.

    The class worked on their journals today. Kate was working very well at the beginning, but then for some reason she started banging on the keys of the keyboard. She said she wasn't angry. Maybe she needed someone's attention. She finished the sentence fine after that. After her lunch and recess, the teacher had her draw a picture in her journal.

    Continuing their discussion about farming, everyone brought in a potato today and the teacher spread out a long sheet of paper on the floor and they peeled potatoes. Most of the kids did really well. Kate surprised herself, I think. She did well, too. They read books, played music, had a square dance, and played "farm" games. Later, when the potatoes were cooked, each child got a scoop of potato and some butter and mashed the potato. Then, one by one, they showed

(continued)

and talked about what they brought to eat that came from a farm. They told how and where it grew (above or below the ground). Everyone got a sample of whatever he or she wanted to try. The day ended with "brown cows" (ice cream sodas) for all. Kate loved every minute. If she was tired today, I couldn't tell. But then, it was such a busy day that she didn't have much time to think about it.

New IEP

Kate's IEP for the following year was determined in an IEP meeting held in June. In part, her IEP stated the following:

Academic Strengths: Can recite Pledge of Allegiance; identifies most body parts; reads 18 of 44 kindergarten sight words; recites alphabet; recognizes capital alphabet letters and 21 lowercase letters; gives rhyming words; recognizes numbers 1–10; names shapes; counts to 29

Academic Weaknesses: Difficulty answering "how many?" questions; doesn't name nickel or dime; not ready for first-grade reading

Behavior Strengths: Names classmates; good attendance; likes attention from classmates and staff

Behavior Weaknesses: Difficulty following directions; distractible

Goals:
- Kate will count orally to 50 at 80 percent accuracy, to be measured quarterly by observation.
- Kate will count orally by 10s to 100 at 80 percent accuracy, to be measured quarterly by observation.
- Kate will answer "how many?" questions when given up to 20 objects to count at 80 percent accuracy, to be measured quarterly by observation.
- Kate will read 8 color words at 80 percent accuracy, to be measured quarterly by observation.
- Kate will read 38 kindergarten and first-grade-level sight words at 80 percent accuracy, to be measured quarterly by observation.
- Kate will not bump into others with her wheelchair as she ambulates down the hallway at 100 percent accuracy, to be measured daily by charting.

- Kate will keep safety belts on her wheelchair buckled at 100 percent accuracy, to be measured daily by charting.
- Kate will use her left hand to support herself when positioned on the floor without prompts and maintain sitting position for 5 minutes, to be measured weekly by observation.
- Kate will use her left hand to protect herself from objects coming at her without prompts, to be measured weekly by observation.
- Kate will use her left hand for personal hygiene needs without prompts (e.g., sneezing, coughing) at 100 percent accuracy, to be measured weekly by observation.
- Kate will pack and unpack her backpack with minimal assistance for 4 out of 5 days, to be measured weekly by observation.

Services:

- 300 minutes per week, August to May: physical impairment services in the special education classroom
- 15 minutes per week, August to May: physical therapy in the special education classroom
- 40 minutes per week, August to May: occupational therapy in the special education classroom
- 1,525 minutes per week, August to May: individual aide in the general education classroom

Case Study Framework Questions

1. What makes this both a contemplation and an exemplar case?
2. How do emotions influence behaviors in the main characters?
3. How is the factual information consistent with current professional literature?
4. Are issues oversimplified? If so, how?
5. Are people stereotyped? If so, how?
6. Discuss teacher dispositions that could facilitate interaction (i.e., self-reflection, tolerance for others, collaboration, multiple perspectives, sound ethical judgment, motivation to work with students with a variety of needs, capacity for advocacy) or that could become a barrier to working with the student discussed in the case.

Thinking Critically About the Case

1. According to the information presented, did Kate learn in kindergarten? How do you know? Give examples.
2. How was the information generated from the daily logs and assessment data used to write Kate's IEP for first grade? Give examples where there were connections.
3. List five accommodations and/or modifications that you would provide for Kate if you were the first-grade teacher.

Activity

Write a lesson on introducing basic addition to first-grade students. Specify how you would modify the lesson to accommodate Kate.

RESOURCES FOR FURTHER INVESTIGATION

Print

Emery, A. (2000). *Muscular dystrophy: The facts* (2nd ed.). New York: Oxford University Press.

Emery, A., & Muntoni, F. (2003). *Duchenne muscular dystrophy* (3rd ed.). New York: Oxford University Press.

Web

March of Dimes Birth Defects Foundation
http://www.marchofdimes.com/

Muscular Dystrophy Association
http://www.mdausa.org

Cystic Fibrosis Foundation
http://www.cff.org/

United Cerebral Palsy
http://www.ucp.org

Chapter 12

Cases Involving Students with Autism and Pervasive Developmental Disorders

CASE **1** **"Max"**

Type of Case: **Contemplation**

Age Level: **High School**

Characters

Max Fuentes, ninth-grade boy

Aaron Fuentes, Max's father

Sylvia Swift, Max's stepmother

Gerry Calvin, ninth-grade history teacher

A Teacher's Reflections

When I found out Max was going to be placed in my ninth-grade U.S. history class, I can't say I was excited. I've been teaching ninth-grade U.S. history for nine years, and I'm pretty comfortable with what I do. I work hard, put a lot into my teaching, try to make adjustments for students with learning disabilities and behavior challenges, engage the students, and generally do a good job of teaching. I work well with the special education teachers and feel comfortable with having their kids in my class. At the end of the year, I always attend the IEP meetings I'm invited to for those students being included in my class. It's nice that the district hires a substitute to cover my class while I'm out for the day at IEP meetings. It's usually a pretty routine procedure. We listen to the eighth-grade teachers discuss the student's progress. The teachers ask the parents if they have any questions or additions. Then the ninth-grade special education teacher discusses goals for the next year and the classes the student will have in special education and/or general education. We all sign our names, and the parents walk out with a stack of papers, looking a little dazed.

Usually, the kids who will be in my classes are your typical students with learning disabilities. The students are bright kids who have trouble with reading, or math, or writing. They need tests read to them, a note taker, books on tape, extended time to finish assignments, big projects broken up, and/or help with organization. Once you have done that type of adjustment for students, it's easy to implement. The first year I had a student in my class who needed modification, it was a different story. I felt unable to meet the student's needs and uneasy about having him in my class. But I worked things out with the special education teacher, and I think our modifications and adaptations have worked well for most of the students.

Max's IEP was different. For one thing, both parents showed up. That's pretty unusual. I am used to seeing one parent or sometimes no parent. Max's stepmom was very quiet, and his dad appeared angry even before we began. It seems that they were at a party recently and overheard a couple of teachers from the junior high talking about their son and his "unusual behavior." The teachers even compared Max to the character in *Rain Man*. To top things off, Aaron Fuentes is a lawyer! He was talking about a parent's right to confidentiality and a breach of ethical behavior. Finally, the principal was called in to talk with Mr. Fuentes. They set up another meeting to talk to the director of special education and the principal from the junior high to discuss the matter. After that, the principal, who usually wanders into an IEP meeting just long enough to sign his name, decided to stay for the whole IEP. I guess every IEP is supposed to have an administrator in attendance.

The rest of the meeting was tense. The teachers started talking about Max's characteristics. This is when I began to get worried. This student wasn't diagnosed with a learning disability. He was diagnosed with pervasive developmental disorder not otherwise specified (PDDNOS). I had never heard that term. When I asked the team to explain the diagnosis, Aaron Fuentes seemed happy to get a chance to share his story. He explained that Max has some but not all of the characteristics associated with autism. Although children with autism have difficulty with verbal and nonverbal communication, have impaired social interactions, engage in repetitive or stereotyped movements, have trouble with change, and have unusual sensory experiences (like being overly sensitive to sound or light), Max has appropriate language skills and no stereotyped movements. However, he does have unusual behaviors, impaired social interactions, and some unusual reactions to sensory stimuli in the environment. It sounded like *Rain Man* to me.

Mr. Fuentes went on to talk about Max's unusual behaviors and his areas of strength. When Max was young, he wasn't able to play in the park until his parents walked around the entire park and touched all of the parking and street signs. This limited their ability to go to big parks because they would spend all of their time walking to touch signs and had no time to play. When Max was a baby, he would organize his toys by size, shape, and color. He wears the same clothes every day. His parents have seven pairs of the same pants and shirts. He refuses to wear shorts or long-sleeve shirts. In the winter, he wears his T-shirt. He will put on a light jacket while he is outside but immediately removes it when he goes in. He also hates shoes and wears sandals all year long. He says shoes make his feet feel too hot. This has led to problems for physical education, because the rules say, "no tennis shoes, no participation in PE." Max doesn't have any "real attachments" to people, according to his parents. Mr. Fuentes told the story about leaving Max for two weeks, when he was three, to go on his honeymoon with Max's stepmother, and Max didn't appear to miss him at all. Max's aunt came to stay with him for two weeks, and he never once asked about his father. When Mr. Fuentes called, Max refused to talk because the phone was too loud. He said this is the hardest thing about having a child with PDDNOS. A couple of weeks ago, Max's little sister walked into the room in a new party dress and Max said, "Nice dress." His eight-year-old sister began to cry because, she said, "It's the first time Max has ever noticed me." She wore the dress again the next day, but Max didn't say anything. On the other hand, Max is almost a genius in history. It's his passion. He can name all the battles fought in the Civil War in alphabetic order and knows the number of casualties recorded for each side. He reads everything he can about war. He even searches the Internet for U.S. troops who are killed in current U.S. missions overseas. It's kind of creepy.

▶▶ **Questions to Ponder**
_____

▶ Whose story is this?

▶ What is my background or previous experience with the issues presented in this case?

▶ What facts are presented?

▶ What opinions are presented?

After Mr. Fuentes talked for a while, the teachers began to talk about Max's progress in Junior High. The team decided that he needed special education services in homeroom and was to be included in the general curriculum for all content courses. His weaknesses were in knowing what to study, remembering due dates, completing assignments, and keeping track of his work and materials. He was reading on grade level, although he had trouble with cause/effect and inference when reading. His math skills were on grade level, and his writing was weak but nothing that required extensive support. When Max got poor grades, it was because he didn't complete work or didn't turn assignments in. Max also had trouble moving between classes. It seems that he only had one route that he walked in the school. He went to each classroom in the order of each period and that was the only route he took. If his schedule for the semester was homeroom, English, math, art, history, PE, and science, and he forgot a book in science, he had to go to all the other rooms before he went to his locker. His parents got Max a rolling backpack in which he carried all of his books and supplies. That way he had all of his stuff with him and never had to use a locker.

When the teachers started talking about what Max would need from his general education teachers, I really felt like this kid was going to be a burden. He needed a study guide sent home two weeks in advance for each test. His parents wanted me to e-mail them every day with his assignments. They wanted books on tape so Max could both read and listen to the book. It was suggested that the teachers use multimedia or PowerPoint lectures to hold Max's interest during the lectures. Plus, Max would carry a calendar to be checked each period by all of his teachers and daily by his parents. Max's dad bought him an electronic organizer for the teachers to record voice direction for assignments, too. It sounded neat, but I would have to spend time learning to program the organizer, which is time I could spend working on other things that would benefit the entire class. Since Max is so interested in history, Mr. Fuentes asked if I could do an independent study project with him to allow him to expand his knowledge. Finally, the parents wanted the teachers to facilitate Max's social development by writing "social stories." They wanted the special education teachers to take pictures of Max with the digital camera showing positive interactions and to write stories about Max in the lunchroom or in the hall that emphasized how he should greet peers, ask questions about their interests, and so forth. They wanted me to develop a social story for history class revolving around the cooperative learning groups I use. It seemed like a lot of work. I am beginning to think Max needs a personal assistant assigned to him like I've seen with students with significant disabilities. An assistant could handle all of these tasks without requiring so much of the teachers, who are already stretched working with all the other students. I think inclusion works for students with mild disabilities but maybe isn't what we need to do for students like Max.

Case Study Framework Questions

1. What makes this a contemplation case?
2. How do emotions influence behaviors in the main characters?
3. How is the factual information consistent with current professional literature?
4. Are issues oversimplified? If so, how?

5. Are people stereotyped? If so, how?
6. Discuss teacher dispositions that could facilitate interaction (i.e., self-reflection, tolerance for others, collaboration, multiple perspectives, sound ethical judgment, motivation to work with students with a variety of needs, capacity for advocacy) or that could become a barrier to working with the student discussed in the case.

Thinking Critically About the Case

1. What did you think about the casual nature of Gerry Calvin's thought process in this case? Did it lead you to speculate about his professional dispositions?
2. What is pervasive developmental disorder not otherwise specified?
3. What accommodations or modifications are the parents asking for within the general education class to support Max?
4. Identify the types of assistive technology described in this case.
5. Would the use of a personal assistant solve the problems that Mr. Calvin described? Why or why not?

Activity

Construct a Venn diagram to compare and contrast the disability categories of autism and pervasive developmental disorder not otherwise specified. Use information from your text, the Internet, and a professional source to construct the Venn diagram.

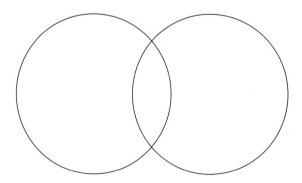

CASE 2 "Rashmi"

Type of Case: Exemplar

Age Level: Elementary School

Characters

Rashmi Shetty, nine-year-old girl diagnosed with autism and a cognitive impairment

Bela and Dipak Shetty, Rashmi's parents

Sagar Shetty, Rashmi's grandfather who lives in her home

Josh Baker, special education teacher

Rashmi Shetty is a nine-year-old girl diagnosed with both autism and a significant cognitive delay. She has no verbal speech and uses a picture board for basic communication skills. Rashmi is in a self-contained special education classroom for students with significant disabilities. There are eight students in the classroom, two paraeducators, and a special education teacher. The special education teacher, Josh Baker, uses positive behavior support (PBS) to reduce inappropriate behavior and teach appropriate behavior.

Positive behavior support is a collaborative assessment-based process developed to provide individualized interventions for individuals with challenging behaviors. The process involves gathering information, developing hypotheses, planning a design, implementing the design, and monitoring the design. The premise of PBS is that individuals with significant disabilities, often with very limited language skills, engage in challenging behavior because it is functional. In other words, it allows them to acquire something or avoid something. An essential part of PBS is functional assessment. Through a functional behavioral assessment, teachers can help identify the intent of the behavior and help students learn positive responses that result in more appropriate behavior. In addition to reducing problem behavior, PBS focuses on improving lifestyle.

Just recently, Rashmi started showing disruptive behaviors for no apparent reason. When she was brought to the table for group work time, she began crying and screaming, hitting herself on the ears, and biting herself on the hands. This behavior was not only self-injurious but also disruptive to the other students. One other student began to cry and scream in response to the sound. Rashmi was immediately removed from the group, but the behavior did not cease.

To gain information about the function of the behavior, Josh Baker decided to begin a functional assessment leading to a positive behavior support plan. The following is information gathered as part of the functional assessment and support plan:

BEHAVIOR JOURNAL

Day 1: Rashmi began crying, screaming, hitting, and biting herself at 10:58 today when she was brought to the paraeducator's desk for group work with three other students. This behavior is very unusual because Rashmi enjoys group work and shows her delight by laughing and smiling when she approaches the table. When comforted by the teacher, Rashmi did not respond as she usually does when upset. The other students in the group became upset, and one began to cry. Rashmi was removed from the group and taken to an individual work center, but the behavior did not decrease. Because of the disruption to the class, Rashmi was taken to the courtyard for a walk. Although she stopped hitting and biting herself, she did not stop crying and screaming. At 12:00, Rashmi was taken to lunch. The behavior stopped at lunch. She ate well and did not exhibit the behavior for the rest of the day.

Day 2: Rashmi began crying, screaming, hitting, and biting herself at 11:15 when working with the teacher and three other students during group work time. Again, Rashmi did not respond when the teacher tried to comfort her. She was taken to the courtyard for a walk. Although she stopped hitting and biting herself, she did not stop crying and screaming. At 12:00, when Rashmi was taken to lunch, the behavior stopped. She ate well and did not display the behavior for the rest of the day.

Day 3: Rashmi began crying, screaming, hitting, and biting herself at 11:08 when working with the teacher and three other students during group work time. Again, Rashmi did not respond when the teacher tried to comfort her. She was taken to the gross motor area to swing (a preferred activity). Although she stopped hitting and biting herself, she did not stop crying and screaming. At 12:00, Rashmi was taken to lunch. She became quiet at lunch, ate all her food, and did not get upset for the rest of the day.

Day 4: Rashmi was not taken to group work time. Instead, she was taken to adaptive physical education at 11:00. Rashmi loves adaptive physical education. She often points to the picture of the PE teacher to request adaptive physical education. Rashmi began crying, screaming, hitting, and biting herself at 11:27. Again, she did not respond when the adaptive PE teacher tried to comfort her. She was taken outside for a walk. However, the behavior worsened. She threw herself on the ground and began kicking. Rashmi was then taken inside to lunch. The behavior stopped. She ate well and did not exhibit the behavior for the rest of the day.

PBS Questions

1. *Who was present when the behavior occurred?* The teacher, three students, and two paraprofessionals. On the fourth day, only the adaptive PE teacher was present.
2. *What was going on when the behavior occurred?* The students were assembled at the desk for group work. On the fourth day, the student was in adaptive PE.
3. *When did the behavior occur?* Between 10:58 and 12:00 each day for four days in a row.
4. *Where did the behavior occur?* In the classroom, the individual work center, the courtyard, the gross motor area, outside, and in the adaptive PE room.
5. *How often did the behavior occur?* Once a day, every day, for four days.
6. *How long did each episode last?* Approximately 30 minutes to an hour.

> ▶▶ **Questions to Ponder**
>
> ▶ Whose story is this?
>
> ▶ What is my background or previous experience with the issues presented in this case?
>
> ▶ What facts are presented?
>
> ▶ What opinions are presented?

Functions of Behavior

There are five general purposes or functions of behavior: to gain attention, to escape or avoid something, to acquire something, to self-regulate, or to play. Josh Baker was able to rule out attention, self-regulation, and play as the function of the behavior. The behavior did not occur when Rashmi was not getting attention, nor did it occur when the teacher or adult stopped paying attention to her. Therefore, attention was eliminated as the purpose of the behavior. Likewise, the behavior was not performed over and over again in a rhythmic or cyclical manner. It did not happen when there was a lot going on or when there was very little going on. Rashmi was unable to perform other actions at the same time as the behavior, so self-regulation was eliminated as the function of the behavior. Play was ruled out, because Rashmi did not seem to enjoy the behavior, nor did she seem to be in her own world while engaged in the behavior. However, Josh was not able to rule out escape/avoidance or acquisition as the purpose of the behavior. The behavior began when Rashmi was in group work time, which might mean she was trying to avoid group work. However, this was untrue on the fourth day, when Rashmi was in adaptive physical education. Rashmi's behavior might also be a function of acquiring food, because the behavior started before lunch on all days and did not continue during lunch. But why did it start happening at this time? To examine the behavior more closely, Josh contacted Rashmi's parents, Bela and Dipak Shetty.

Bela and Dipak Shetty are the parents of four children. Rashmi is their oldest child; the other children are seven, three, and one. Rashmi's paternal grandfather, Sagar Shetty, also lives with the family. Rashmi and her grandfather have a very close relationship. He has taken on the responsibility of assisting Rashmi with many of her daily living needs. He is typically the person who wakes Rashmi, gets her ready for school, assists her in eating, takes her to school, and puts her to bed at night. Eating is a challenge for Rashmi. She has many sensory issues, and the texture of most foods makes her gag. She is unable to eat anything creamy, cold, lumpy, or varied in texture. Her preference is for crunchy foods. Because of her eating difficulty, it often takes her an hour to finish each meal. With three younger children, Bela Shetty is glad to have the assistance of her father-in-law.

Sagar recently was able to travel back to his home country of India for a visit. Dipak Shetty, a college professor, was going to work late to help his wife get the children ready for school. However, last week was finals week, and he had to be on campus early. Bela and Sagar hypothesized that Rashmi's behavior might have been due to hunger. Since Bela was the only adult getting the children up and ready, Rashmi wasn't getting personal attention during breakfast. She may have been eating less and so might have been hungry earlier in the day.

Josh Baker agreed that hunger might be causing the behavior. He decided not to take Rashmi to lunch early because she would miss group time, which she usually enjoys. Instead, Josh assigned one of the paraeducators to give Rashmi pretzels around 10:30. Because the pretzels are crunchy, she was able to eat them independently and then participate in group work at 11:00.

Case Study Framework Questions

1. What makes this an exemplar case?
2. How do emotions influence behaviors in the main characters?
3. How is the factual information consistent with current professional literature?
4. Are issues oversimplified? If so, how?
5. Are people stereotyped? If so, how?
6. Discuss teacher dispositions that could facilitate interaction (i.e., self-reflection, tolerance for others, collaboration, multiple perspectives, sound ethical judgment, motivation to work with students with a variety of needs, capacity for advocacy) or that could become a barrier to working with the student discussed in the case.

Thinking Critically About the Case

1. Using the PBS questions, describe Rashmi's behavior in objective terms.
2. What are positive behavior supports?
3. Why was 10:30 selected as the time for snack?
4. What are the strengths and weaknesses of Josh Baker's plan for Rashmi?
5. If the behavior continues, what do you think could be causing it?
6. What should happen when Rashmi's grandfather returns?

Activity

Using the Internet, search for the terms *functional behavioral assessment* and *positive behavior supports*. Write a review of three articles you found that were well written and contained relevant information.

RESOURCES FOR FURTHER INVESTIGATION

Print

Buitelaar, J., Gagg, V., & Rutger, J. (1998). Diagnostic rules for children with PDD-NOS and multiple complex developmental disorder. *Journal of Child Psychology and Psychiatry and Allied Disciplines, 39*(6), 911–920.

McDougle, C. J., Kresch, L. E., & Posey, D. J. (2000). Repetitive thoughts and behavior in pervasive developmental disorders: Treatment with serotonin reuptake inhibitors. *Journal of Autism and Developmental Disorders, 30*(5), 427–435.

Mirenda, P. (2001). Autism, augmentative communication, and assistive technology: What do we really know? *Focus on Autism and Other Developmental Disabilities, 16*(3), 141–151.

Portway, S., & Johnson, B. (2003). Asperger syndrome and the children who "don't quite fit in." *Early Child Development and Care, 173*(4), 435–443.

Quinn, B., & Malone, A. (2000). *Pervasive developmental disorders: An altered perspective*. Philadelphia: Jessica Kingsley.

Simpson, R. L., DeBoer-Ott, S. R., & Smith-Myles, B. (2003). Inclusion of learners with autism spectrum disorders in general education settings. *Topics in Language Disorders, 23*(2), 116–133.

Starr, E. M., Foy, J. B., & Cramer, K. M. (2001). Parental perceptions of the education of children with pervasive developmental disorders. *Education and Training in Mental Retardation and Developmental Disabilities, 36*(1), 55–68.

Waltz, M. (1999). *Pervasive developmental disorders: Diagnosis, options, and answers*. Arlington, TX: Future Horizon.

Zager, D. (2004). *Autism spectrum disorder*. Manhattan, MA: Pace University.

Web

Autism Center
http://www.patientcenters.com/autism/

Autism Society of America
http://www.autism-society.org

Autism Spectrum Disorders (Pervasive Developmental Disorders)
http://www.nimh.nih.gov/publicat/autism.cfm

Chapter 13

Cases Involving Students with Traumatic Brain Injury

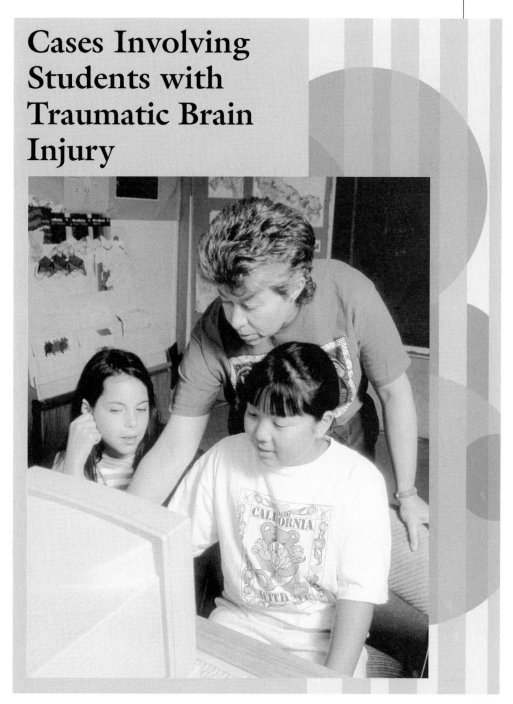

Case 1 "Gustavo"

Type of Case: Exemplar

Age Level: High School

Characters

Gustavo Martinez, twelfth-grade student

Andrea Martinez, Gustavo's mother

Ginny Lopez, high school Spanish teacher

Mike Putnam, high school special education teacher

High school kids do crazy things. Andrea had even done some pretty dumb things in her day. But this seemed so senseless. She wondered if he even thought about the consequences of his actions. She wondered if he knew what happened. She wondered why it had happened to him and how she would get through this.

He was born on a sunny spring day. She was young. Maybe even too young to be ready for a baby, but there he was, that little squirming bundle with a head full of brown hair. And she loved him immediately. Being a single mother at eighteen wasn't easy, but they had found their way through life together. However, she had been through tough times. When her husband, Alonzo, died in a car accident, she didn't think she could go on. Soon after Alonzo died, she found she was expecting a baby. As her child grew, she learned to depend on him. Gus got his first job at fifteen, and she depended on him for money as well as support. He was as much her friend as her son. In school, he had always gotten by. Many of his teachers described him as impulsive and reckless. Some of his teachers even suggested that he should be tested for attention deficit disorder, but Andrea just thought he was a normal, active boy with a lot of energy. At times he could be hard to control, but they really didn't have too many rules at home, and that suited both of them well. Besides, she didn't have much use for those special education teachers. She had been tested in school and put into a class for retarded kids for two years until the school figured out that she wasn't retarded, just that she didn't speak English too well.

As Gus entered high school, he started to run with a different crowd, and Andrea suspected that he was using drugs occasionally. But didn't most kids that age? He was still passing his classes, although English and biology were borderline, and he had a full-time job. He acted like an adult, so maybe he needed some time to relax and blow off some steam. Things seemed to be going pretty well, and then her life changed.

She received the news at 11:50 on a Friday night when an officer came to her door. Andrea knew immediately that something was very wrong. She knew Gus was going out to party that night. It sounded like a harmless prank. They lived in a small town with a town square and a fountain in the middle of it. Gus and his friends had decided to put soap bubbles in the water. They had been drinking. It wasn't a big deal until Gus decided to pry the electrical box out of the bottom of the fountain with a screwdriver he had in his truck. He was the only one in the fountain or the other kids could have been electrocuted also. But the kids were afraid to get in the water to pull him out. The police officer told her that it was electrocution and a near drowning. He was "down" for several minutes before the medical technicians arrived with the ambulance. He was literally brought back to life. When she got to the hospital, he was in a coma but breathing on his own. They told her that he had probably sustained permanent brain damage. He had been without oxygen for quite a while. If he came out of the coma, they weren't sure what he would be like. All she could do was wait.

▶▶ Questions to Ponder

▶ Whose story is this?

▶ What is my background or previous experience with the issues presented in this case?

▶ What facts are presented?

▶ What opinions are presented?

Andrea waited and worried. Would he come out of the coma? What would he be like? How could she take care of him? How would she pay her daily bills without his help? How would she pay the hospital bills?

A week later he came out of the coma. He was still using a catheter and was being tube-fed. But he was blinking and responding to pain. Andrea thought sometimes his eyes would follow her across the room. She was there every day and spent as much time as she could.

Two months went by, and she was told that his condition was stabilized. He would have to be released from the hospital and she would need to make arrangements for his care. The thought of sending him away was more than she could stand. They had been together for seventeen years. There had to be another way.

One evening in the hospital, Ginny Lopez, the high school Spanish teacher, and Mike Putnam, who introduced himself as the special education teacher, visited Andrea and Gus. This was the first contact Andrea had had from anyone at school. Even Gus's friends didn't come to visit. Andrea remembered Ginny Lopez. She laughed as Ginny told a story about how Gus had decided to take Spanish for an "easy A" until he found out that he had to read and write Spanish as well as speak it. Ginny told about Gus's efforts to distract the class. Once he put fire-crackers in a bull piñata that hung in the back of the room and lit it, blowing the bull's horns across the room. He didn't mean to destroy the piñata; he just wasn't thinking. Andrea remembered that Gus was surprised that Ms. Lopez hadn't sent him to the office.

Ginny Lopez explained that she asked Mike Putnam to come along because he was a special education teacher in the district. Andrea immediately didn't trust him. Those kinds of teachers were all alike. They came in and tested kids for a few hours and then thought they were the experts on everything. He didn't have anything that Andrea wanted to hear. He was probably going to tell her about some institution where they send kids like Gustavo. He didn't understand that Gus wasn't like those kids. He might get better. The doctors couldn't tell her that he wouldn't. She knew he had "brain damage," but maybe it could be fixed. But Ms. Lopez had brought him, so she would listen to him.

Mr. Putnam asked if Andrea thought about Gus's transition back to school. The use of the word *school* surprised her. What was he thinking? Gus wore diapers, he couldn't sit in a desk, he couldn't move on his own, and he couldn't even speak. What in the world would he do at school? Then Mike Putnam began to describe a program for students with disabilities. He told her that the students were brought to school on a special bus with a lift, and they were pushed in wheelchairs to the classroom. Several students sat in beanbag chairs or stood in standing boards, and one student had a hospital bed at school. The teachers and assistants changed the student's diapers and fed some students using feeding tubes just like at the hospital. The students received physical therapy, vision therapy, music therapy, and other services, if needed. The teachers worked on skills like visual tracking, using assistive technology for communication, and motor control. She couldn't believe what she heard. This was much better than an institution or a nursing home.

"Would a school like this be able to make Gus better?" she asked. "The doctors say that Gus has brain damage and that he probably isn't going to get better but they aren't sure. Could this school make him better?"

Mike Putnam spoke slowly. "I wish I could say yes," he began. "Most of the students in the school make some progress, but it is very slow and some make no progress at all. I don't know about Gus, but I can tell you that we will work with him. We will give him the support he needs and help you with his transition from high school to a community setting."

How much would this cost, she wondered? She could barely afford to pay her rent, much less the medical bills. There was no way she could pay for this special school.

Case Study Framework Questions

1. What makes this an exemplar case?
2. How do emotions influence behaviors in the main characters?
3. How is the factual information consistent with current professional literature?
4. Are issues oversimplified? If so, how?
5. Are people stereotyped? If so, how?
6. Discuss teacher dispositions that could facilitate interaction (i.e., self-reflection, tolerance for others, collaboration, multiple perspectives, sound ethical judgment, motivation to work with students with a variety of needs, capacity for advocacy) or that could become a barrier to working with the student discussed in the case.

Thinking Critically About the Case

1. What happened to Gus that left him with a disability?
2. Describe the relationship between Gus and his mother.
3. What does this case say about "zero reject" and "free appropriate public education"?
4. Should school districts have to provide these types of intensive services for students with severe or multiple disabilities? Why or why not?

Activity

As a group, evaluate the case. What was happening? What was going well and not so well? What additional information would be useful to better understand the situation? What could have been done differently? As a group, choose volunteers to reenact the discussion between Andrea Martinez, Ginny Lopez, and Mike Putnam.

CASE 2 "Andrew"

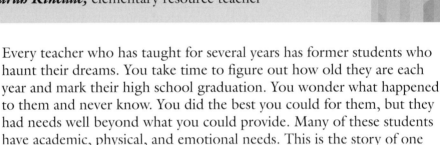

Type of Case: Contemplation

Age Level: Elementary School

Characters

> *Drew Douglas,* former elementary student diagnosed with
> traumatic brain injury

> *Sarah Kincade,* elementary resource teacher

Every teacher who has taught for several years has former students who haunt their dreams. You take time to figure out how old they are each year and mark their high school graduation. You wonder what happened to them and never know. You did the best you could for them, but they had needs well beyond what you could provide. Many of these students have academic, physical, and emotional needs. This is the story of one such student.

I knew Andrew Douglas well before he put a foot inside Southside Elementary School. I had testified at the trial involving his older sister, Faith, when she was a second-grader and Andrew was just a toddler. I knew Faith because she was diagnosed with a learning disability in my classroom. Her home situation was problematic, and the school principal had called the Division of Family Services (DFS) on several occasions about possibilities of child abuse. Faith had marks ranging from bruises to burns. Then there was the inappropriate behavior, such as masturbating in class, drawing explicit pictures, and talking of sexual acts. Faith was taken out of the home and placed in foster care in the middle of second grade, and her father was charged with physical and sexual abuse. However, there was no indication of child abuse against Andrew, so he remained in the home. Two months after Faith was taken out of the home, Andrew hovered near death in a hospital with a skull fracture. The school staff were devastated when they heard what had happened on the local news. We had all questioned the decision to leave Andrew in the home, but we had no control over it. Then I lost touch with the case until a small, red-haired boy with freckles and a bright smile walked into Southside Elementary to attend kindergarten. I knew immediately who he was because he looked so much like Faith.

At the time, Andrew was living with his mother and grandmother. His mother and father had gotten a divorce and his father was in jail. His mother had gone through counseling and had worked to get Andrew back when he recovered from his injury. She had moved out of state for a while but decided to move home when Andrew entered kindergarten so he could attend the same school that she had gone to.

Right away the kindergarten teachers worried about Andrew's academic skills. Andrew had difficulty with memory. He might identify a circle on one day and then be unable to recognize or name the shape the next day. He had difficulty with word finding. He used language that would explain but didn't name. For instance, he might say, "Last night we went to that place with the yellow thing, those things that go up and down, that have the um . . . arches. You know, that place to eat hamburgers." He also seemed to change emotions quickly. One minute he was as happy as could be and the next minute he would be crying because he couldn't find a book. He was also impulsive and unable to concentrate. It seemed that he tried to attend to everything in the environment at once. While he was listening to the story he would also be looking outside, listening to the fan, watching the other children, and looking for chips in the floor tile.

Andrew was referred to the Teacher Assistance Team in our building, and the kindergarten teacher documented the modification made in the classroom. After three months, he was referred for an evaluation. At that point I became directly involved in Andrew's case. I knew his mother from my previous IEP meetings for Faith. She seemed happy that I was working with Andrew. She agreed to provide a medical history for Andrew, and we requested copies of his medical records with her permission. From the medical records, we found Andrew had suffered a skull fracture and retinal hemorrhages, and the doctors suspected shaken baby syndrome as well as the blunt trauma for which he was hospitalized. Andrew qualified for special education services under the category of traumatic brain injury and was placed in my resource classroom for services.

▶▶ **Questions to Ponder**

▶ Whose story is this?

▶ What is my background or previous experience with the issues presented in this case?

▶ What facts are presented?

▶ What opinions are presented?

Andrew was a sweet little boy with significant academic needs. He also appeared so emotionally needy. Although the signs of physical and sexual abuse that I had seen in Faith were not present with Andrew, there were signs of neglect. He would come to school dirty and hungry most mornings. He devoured anything we had to eat at school. He was very quiet about anything going on at home and once told me his mom said, "We keep our family stuff to ourselves." He loved to listen to books and would often try to crawl up into my lap as I read. Although he loved the books, he couldn't remember them from day to day. He couldn't name the students in the class at the end of the year, and he couldn't recognize any letters in the alphabet or numerals even after intensive small-group instruction for several months. Andrew didn't even recognize his own name or the letters in his name. And as more vocabulary was introduced in school, his word-finding difficulties became worse. He began seeing the speech/language pathologist for individual therapy twice a week. Yet, Andrew could do things to surprise me as well. He was a talented artist and drew amazing pictures of animals. He could do puzzles and loved the computer. I tried to get computer programs to teach reading. Although he tried, he just couldn't learn letters or words.

The interesting thing about being a resource special education teacher is that you get to have students for several years. I had Andrew for six years, from kindergarten through fifth grade. I saw him every day for about two hours. His mother moved in and out of his life. Then one day in fourth grade, Andrew's mother and grandmother got into a fistfight and they were kicked out of his grandmother's house. After that, Andrew lived in the car with his mother. Even though I called DFS on several occasions, nothing was done to remove Andrew from this situation. His mother used to drop Andrew off at a fast food restaurant at 6:00 in the morning. He would wait there until 8:30 and then walk to the school five blocks away. I arranged for a mother in the neighborhood to let Andrew go there and sleep on the couch before school, because he seemed so tired by 8:30.

The thing about Andrew that haunts me is how sweet and kind he was despite his situation. He was the first child to praise another and the first child to comfort a friend in trouble. He never spoke an unkind word to anyone in the six years that I knew him, yet I knew he had heard many unkind words. He helped me carry books and would open doors for everyone. On the last day of sixth grade, I had car duty. I stood outside to make sure all the students got picked up after school. Andrew's mother was late, so he was the last one left. We talked about going to middle school and his plans. I told him that I wanted him to come and visit me next year. He told me that he might be moving but he wasn't sure where. Finally, after an hour, his mother pulled up in a car with plastic wrap on the windows. Andrew got inside, and as they were driving away he pulled back the plastic and leaned out of the window waving. Then he shouted, "I love you Mrs. Kincade. Thanks!" And that was the last time I ever saw Andrew Douglas. But, it isn't the last time I will think of Andrew.

I will always wonder if I could have done more to help him. I did, eventually, teach him to read at about the second-grade level. I bought him tennis shoes and a winter coat every year, which I said came from Goodwill. I made sure he had a safe place to sleep at school when he needed it, and sometimes he needed sleep more than education. I tried to nurture him without crossing the boundaries between teacher and student. Andrew will be nineteen this year, and I wonder where he is and what he is doing. I can only hope the best for the sweet, bright-eyed, little boy who haunts my dreams from time to time.

Case Study Framework Questions

1. What makes this a contemplation case?
2. How do emotions influence behaviors in the main characters?
3. How is the factual information consistent with current professional literature?
4. Are issues oversimplified? If so, how?
5. Are people stereotyped? If so, how?
6. Discuss teacher dispositions that could facilitate interaction (i.e., self-reflection, tolerance for others, collaboration, multiple perspectives, sound ethical judgment, motivation to work with students with a variety of needs, capacity for advocacy) or that could become a barrier to working with the student discussed in the case.

Thinking Critically About the Case

1. What caused Andrew's traumatic brain injury?
2. What characteristics of traumatic brain injury does Andrew exhibit?
3. How could word-finding problems affect a child's academic progress?
4. Shaken baby syndrome accounts for an estimated 10 to 12 percent of all deaths due to abuse and neglect in the United States. What could schools do to help prevent this type of child abuse?
5. How does child abuse and child neglect differ?

Activity

Using the Internet, research signs of child abuse that teachers need to be aware of. Write a reflective paper describing the signs of child abuse and the legal obligations teachers face in reporting suspected instances of child abuse.

RESOURCES FOR FURTHER INVESTIGATION

Print

Chapman, S. B., & McKinnon, L. (2000). Discussion of developmental plasticity: Factors affecting cognitive outcome after pediatric traumatic brain injury. *Journal of Communication Disorders, 33*(4), 333–344.

Hunt, N., & Marshall, K. (2002). *Exceptional children and youth* (3rd ed.). Boston: Houghton Mifflin.

Kendall, E., & Murphy, P. (2003). The determinants of work adjustment following traumatic brain injury: A focus for career counselors. *Australian Journal of Career Development, 12*(1), 25–35.

Keyser-Marcus, L., Briel, L., Sherron-Targett, P., Yasuda, S., Johnson, S., & Wehman, P. (2002). Enhancing the schooling of students with traumatic brain injury. *Teaching Exceptional Children, 34*(4), 62–67.

Plotts, C. (2002). Recognizing LD, ADHD and TBI in adults. *Adult Learning, 12*(2), 5–7.

Truman, P. (2004). Problems in identifying cases of child neglect. *Nursing Standard, 18*(29), 33–39.

Web

Brain Injury in Children
http://www.braininjury.com/children.html

Child Abuse
http://childabuse.com

General Information about Traumatic Brain Injury
http://www.kidsource.com/NICHCY/brain.html

Chapter **14**

Cases Involving Students with Attention Deficit Hyperactivity Disorder

CASE 1 "John"

Type of Case: Contemplation

Age Level: Middle School

Characters

John Brooks, twelve-year-old boy who has the health impairment of attention deficit hyperactivity disorder (ADHD)

Mrs. Brooks, his mother

Mrs. Brooks showed a look of concern as her twelve-year-old son, John, raced past her and up the stairs to his room. "John," she said, "Are you OK?" She heard John's bedroom door close. She quietly walked upstairs and entered his room. John sat in a chair staring at the TV. She turned the TV off and asked, "Did something happen?" John stared silently at the TV for what seemed several minutes. Mrs. Brooks calmly said, "John, I know that you can handle yourself and make good decisions, but sometimes help or support from an adult is necessary. If you feel you need help, I know you will let me know." John sat quietly, so Mrs. Brooks left the room.

Later that day, John walked into the kitchen and said to his mother, "They took my new skate shoes." Mrs. Brooks sat down at the kitchen table as she said, "Who?" John then conveyed a long story about riding on his skateboard to the school and seeing a group of seventh-grade boys with whom John wanted to be friends. They practiced on their skateboards for a while, and then John took off his shoes to do something on the skateboard. When he turned around to get his shoes, they were gone and so were the other kids. He then walked home.

Mrs. Brooks made a list of boys who were at the school and contacted each parent to tell them what had occurred and to request help in locating the shoes. Twenty minutes later, a parent drove up and two boys got out. They met John and Mrs. Brooks at the front door and gave the shoes back to John as they apologized.

This was just another incident in a long history of incidents with the same group of boys. They just didn't like John and were not kind to him. Just two weeks ago, one boy met John every day at his locker and called him "stupid" and made fun of him. John never reacted, but

Mrs. Brooks knew he felt alone. John was never invited to any other child's house, and the boys wouldn't allow him to sit at their lunch table. Mrs. Brooks recognized that John was dealing with emotional abuse, but she was afraid to say much to John's teachers or the principal for fear that the boys would make it even more difficult for John.

From the time he was a young child, John was always verbal, intelligent, and somewhat disorganized. He also experienced difficulty making and keeping friends. In retrospect, John's behavior suggested some signs of ADHD very early in life. Even as a baby, he was irritable and always in motion. He talked early, and his language skills were very sophisticated. However, as a toddler, he behaved in an impulsive and driven manner. One time, he even slapped his cousin! Another time, Mrs. Brooks overheard her sister-in-law talking to another relative about how sorry she felt for Mrs. Brooks because of John's behavior. These occurrences caused great stress and a rift in the family. Mrs. Brooks worked with John on countless behavior charts with rewards and consequences. Although frustrated, John always responded positively to this kind of system.

In school, the teachers viewed John as academically capable but a challenge. In kindergarten, as other children built Lego creations, John impulsively knocked the creations apart. In first grade, it was difficult for John to focus on the task at hand and control his impulsivity. For example, when the children lined up for lunch, John pushed his way to the front of the line. By second grade, children avoided John and he experienced few friendships. In third grade, John became easily frustrated with written language skills, and often his handwriting and spelling skills were poor. The third-grade teacher suggested a tutor to teach cursive writing. By fourth grade, John was evaluated for attention deficit hyperactivity disorder at his mother's insistence. John's teacher completed an attention deficit disorders rating scale, which indicated problems with attending and impulsivity. John's mother worked with the school nurse and social worker to provide health and social history information. Ultimately, John was prescribed Ritalin by his physician, which helped with his impulsivity and level of focus. In an IEP meeting, he was labeled "Other Health Impaired," and his IEP focused on adaptations in the classroom as well as consultation between the special education teacher and the regular education teacher. Fortunately, John improved greatly in all academic areas, but he still experienced difficulty relating to other children.

▶▶ **Questions to Ponder**

▶ Whose story is this?

▶ What is my background or previous experience with the issues presented in this case?

▶ What facts are presented?

▶ What opinions are presented?

Mrs. Brooks recalled the last IEP meeting for John. Working with his teachers seemed challenging and frustrating. As she talked about the other boys harassing John in the hallway and calling him names, the teachers' response was, "Boys will be boys," and "They will grow out of it," and "We never see anything happen in the classroom." John needed to have notes provided before a class lecture and to have preferential seating. Although his special education teacher assisted John by helping with organizational skills, the teachers were inconsistent about providing accommodations. For example, one teacher said he didn't have time to provide notes before lectures, and another teacher often forgot to provide preferential seating. One teacher questioned if John really had ADHD and only reluctantly placed John in the front row in class. Although the IEP meeting was frustrating, John was slowly experiencing more success. He was earning an A in literature, a B in science, and a C in math and English. He also continued to participate in band and chorus and was a talented soccer player. Just as important, John developed several new friendships from his soccer team outside the school. He even made several close friendships with a girl in another grade and a new boy in his grade.

In the end, Mrs. Brooks decided not to challenge the teachers because she was afraid that John would experience some retaliation from them if she confronted them about these issues. However, she was determined to be more assertive in making sure that John was not subjected to harassment. Since her telephone call to parents about the shoe incident, the boys had stopped verbally harassing John. She resolved to encourage John to stay involved in activities that did not involve the boys who harassed him, like music, soccer and track. She also continued to provide emotional support and to encourage John to play with neighborhood children. After all, in one year, John would be ready for high school, and he would have an opportunity to make friends with other students.

Case Study Framework Questions

1. What makes this a contemplation case?
2. How do emotions influence behaviors in the main characters?
3. How is the factual information consistent with current professional literature?
4. Are issues oversimplified? If so, how?
5. Are people stereotyped? If so, how?
6. Discuss teacher dispositions that could facilitate interaction (i.e., self-reflection, tolerance for others, collaboration, multiple perspectives, sound ethical judgment, motivation to work with students with a variety of needs, capacity for advocacy) or that could become a barrier to working with the student discussed in this case.

Thinking Critically About the Case

1. What accommodations and modifications were made for John in the regular education classroom?
2. Why do you think some accommodations and modifications were inconsistently carried out in the regular classroom?
3. For those accommodations and modifications inconsistently carried out, what could the regular education teachers have done to be consistent?
4. What are the consequences for not carrying out the accommodations and modifications?
5. How could the IEP process have been used to discuss issues of emotional abuse?
6. What other professionals should be involved, and what should they be doing?

Activity

If a child is subjected to emotional abuse from other students, what can you, as a classroom teacher, do to help? With a partner, brainstorm at least ten ideas that might be helpful and useful.

CASE 2 "Jerry"

Type of Case: Contemplation

Age Level: High School

Characters

>*Jerry Basco,* fifteen-year-old student with disabilities (attention deficit hyperactivity disorder and emotional disorder)

>*Mary Basco,* Jerry's mother

>*Andy Kova,* assistant principal

>*Peggy Meuth,* English teacher

Note: You will read about this student from four different perspectives and then review the student's Functional Behavioral Assessment and Behavior Intervention Plan.

Jerry

The only time I remember liking school was in eighth grade when we had the school play. Our class performed *Guys and Dolls* and I had a part, as a gambler. We got out of class to practice, and we had practice every night. I liked it when the audience clapped at the end of the play. It was also one of the only times I can remember my mom not being mad at me.

About two months before the play began, I got in big trouble in the neighborhood. I went to a kid's house after school and stole $50 from his room. I didn't think I'd get caught, because there was no way to trace the money, but the kid's dad found me in the school parking lot after I took it and told me he knew I had the money. Even then, I denied it, but the kid's dad saw the money sticking out from my sock. He called my mom and I was in big trouble.

Now I'm in high school and high school sucks. It's worse than grade school. I'm fifteen and my mom won't let me take driver's ed because of my grades. I especially hate my English teacher. She's always after me, looking for me to do something wrong. Just the other day, she gave me a lecture about not doing my homework and I told her to "shut up." She kicked me out of class and the principal suspended me for the day. I got in trouble at home. I get tired of people telling me that I need to pay attention in class and that I have a "bad attitude."

That principal is also after me. Even when I walk down the hallway, he tells me to "pull my pants up, my boxers are showing." One time, he made me put on a rope belt! Man, that was embarrassing. That principal is also always on me to get to class on time, but when can I talk to my friends? Also, if he had to have an individual aide shadowing him all the time, he'd be upset too. It really sucks having another adult walking me to class and sitting in class with me.

I'm also sick of people making me see a psychiatrist because I have some stupid illness: bipolar and ADHD, whatever that is. They make me take medicine, even though I told them it doesn't help. Other people are my problem. If they would just leave me alone and quit bothering me, I would do better.

▶▶ Questions to Ponder

▶ Whose story is this?

▶ What is my background or previous experience with the issues presented in this case?

▶ What facts are presented?

▶ What opinions are presented?

Mrs. Meuth

There is only so much I can do with a student like Jerry. I teach 150 students every day, and if they were all like Jerry, I would quit. I know Jerry has many problems and that his mother is trying hard to help. He has also been assigned an individual aide throughout the day to make sure he gets to class on time and to help in class, but I don't really think this has helped. Jerry walks into class every day with a "chip on his shoulder." He constantly fidgets in class, tapping a pencil, looking around the room, playing with the zipper on his backpack. One day, he threw paper spitwads at students while taking a test. He pays attention for about the first 5 minutes of class, and then begins to bother other students. He makes rude comments and talks out while the other students laugh at him. He is completely disorganized. His books and papers are often in a huge stack, and he usually doesn't even have a pen. He rushes through an assignment and then bothers other students. He rarely completes any homework. The other day, I talked to him about homework. I started to tell him that if only he would complete the homework, he could easily pass this class. He looked at me and told me to shut up! I just can't take this kind of behavior in my class, so I sent him to the principal and he was suspended. If Jerry would only think before he speaks, he wouldn't make half the rude comments he does. I really think Jerry has good potential, but he just doesn't apply himself. He can write, but he gets so angry and frustrated when I tell him he has to edit his work. His spelling and handwriting skills are very poor, but when I tell him to use a word processor to write, he gets angry. If he raises his hand in class and I don't immediately call on him, he shouts out an answer. I just can't keep control of my class and teach English with someone like Jerry in class.

Mrs. Basco

I'm just frantic about Jerry. He seems to be going downhill fast. I'm now taking him to see the psychiatrist weekly and he is taking Zoloft and Ritalin, but he is still in trouble every day at school. Maybe a full day of school is too much for him. Jerry has always been difficult, even when he was a baby. He was irritable and cried all the time. As he became older, he was always active, running and talking all the time. We visited the emergency room on numerous occasions because of cuts, burns, and other accidents. He was always on "full speed." His fifth-grade teacher suggested that I have him evaluated for ADHD, and I'm glad I did. Not only was he diagnosed with ADHD, but he also has bipolar disorder. He is very impulsive and goes from running nonstop to not being able to get out of bed to go to school. Lately, he has been coming home from school extremely upset, and the other day he was suspended for talking back to a teacher. I'm trying to handle him as best I can, but it's becoming more difficult. I am a single parent and I get home every day at 6:00 P.M. I am just running out of energy. I really don't think the school works well with Jerry, either. I insisted that they have a full-time aide with him, and this helped for a few weeks. But after that Jerry was late to every class, and after five tardies he was placed in in-school suspension. During in-school suspension, Jerry talked out and was given additional days of in-school suspension. Then he eventually was suspended out of school. The original offense was being tardy for class, and he ended up spending more time out of class than in class!

Mr. Kova

What a day! This is my first year as assistant principal at this high school. I've dealt with many issues, but this is one of the most severe. I must write the incident so that it can be considered at an expulsion hearing.

INCIDENT REPORT

On September 15, at approximately 8:20 A.M., Jerry Basco was sent to the office for calling me a "f#*## b*#**" in the physical education locker room where the PE teacher could hear. The PE teacher informed me of the incident when he brought Jerry to the office. I walked to where Jerry was waiting in the front office and asked if he called me that name. Jerry said, "yes." I asked him what had him so angry. He gave me a letter, which was part of an assignment written by another student, and he said that was the reason why he was so angry. I read the letter, which was written by another student and included unkind statements about Jerry, and I told him he would be going to the Alternative Room for referring to me with profanity. He then said he wanted to be suspended and used more profanity. I told him to cool down as we walked with his individual special education aide to his locker to get his books for the Alternative Room. He said, using profanity, that he wasn't moving until he got his letter back. I told him he wouldn't get it back because it wasn't his; it was the other student's letter. He continued to curse and say that he wasn't moving until he got his letter. I went to tell the principal about the situation. He asked Jerry what the problem was. Jerry again said that he wanted his letter back. The principal told him to get control and that the letter wasn't his so he wouldn't get it back. He told Jerry to stop cursing or he would be suspended for ten days. Jerry said, "What are you going to do about it, old man?" and moved toward the principal as if he were trying to provoke him. The principal told me to call the police, which I did. Jerry was then told that he would be removed by the police from school grounds if he didn't get himself together. Jerry continued to use profanity and threatened to bring the whole school down and sue me for all that I've got. The police arrived quickly and instructed Jerry to stop causing a scene and to go with them. Jerry continued to yell about his lawyer and left with the police.

JERRY'S FUNCTIONAL BEHAVIORAL ASSESSMENT AND BEHAVIOR INTERVENTION PLAN FOR THE CURRENT SCHOOL YEAR

FUNCTIONAL BEHAVIORAL ASSESSMENTS/BEHAVIORAL INTERVENTION PLANS

I. **Problem Identification**

   A. Student's Strengths and Interests

      _____ Good sense of humor, creative thinker, likes sports, likes to read aloud in class, polite in one-to-one situations with adults, has potential for leadership, polite in class 70% of time _____

      _____

      _____

   B. List All the Child's Behaviors of Concern

      _____ Jerry exhibits inappropriate comments directed toward students and staff including rude comments, disruptive and loud comments that interrupt learning in the classroom; comments that provoke others; blurting out including singing and off-task comments; cursing—occurs more than once a week to more than once per hour—Consequence can be detention, but generally mild; Behavior lasts less than one minute or until redirected—Jerry is frequently late for class resulting in detention and suspensions _____

      _____

      _____

   C. Prioritize Behaviors with Selected Target Behavior on Line 1.

      1. Tardies

      2. Dress code violations (pants far below waist)

      3. Appropriate comments

   D. Previous Interventions

Intervention (include reinforcement schedule)	Date Started	Date Ended	Reason Ended
Verbal reminder—aide to get to class on time	8/20		
Verbal warning about detentions—daily—aide	8/20		

(continued)

E. Determine Any Long-Term Antecedents That May Affect Behavior

_____ Jerry is diagnosed with ADHD and Bi-Polar Disorder; takes medication; is anxious and sometimes depressed; doesn't sleep well; doesn't make or keep friends easily

F. Determine the Antecedent and Consequent Events Surrounding the Behavior (provide documentation)

Antecedent	Behavior	Consequence
___ Give assignment	___ Rude comment	___ Verbal reprimand
___ Transition from class to class	___ Dawdles; talks to others	___ Tardy to class
___ Walk down hall	___ Pants below waist	___ Must put on belt and pull pants up

G. Identify the Function of the Behavior

Behavior	Communicative Function	Appropriate Replacement Behavior
___ Rude comments	___ Gain attention from peers and teachers; anger release	___ No comments
___ Transition— tardy to class— dawdles—talks to others	___ Gain attention; go to office	___ Get to class on time
___ Pants below waist	___ Gain attention; go to office	___ Pants above waist

H. Describe the Desired Behavior (replacement behavior, objective description, and measurable terms. For example, during math class, will raise his hand before he talks 90% of the time.)

___ When given an assignment, Jerry will not make any verbal comments.
___ Jerry will arrive at each class on-time.
___ Jerry will wear pants above his waist 90% of the time.

_____

_____

II. Plan and Implementation

A. Brainstorm Possible Solutions (environment, curriculum, behavior)

_____

      ___ Meet with Human Support Center Counselor weekly
      ___ Aide will reinforce appropriate behavior (e.g., verbal praise)
      ___ Teachers/staff will give verbal praise for appropriate behavior
      ___ Parents will be contacted when Jerry has a good day

B. Procedure for Implementation

  1. What happens if desired behavior occurs? (State types of reinforcers and schedule.) _____

    a. Jerry (and aide) may leave the classroom if frustration is too much to handle and go to an empty room for a 5-minute "cool off" time _____

    b. Aide will use proximity control and move closer if a problem occurs

  2. What happens if desired behavior does not occur? (Include consequences and prompting.)

    Verbal prompts—aide, teacher _____

  3. What are the criteria for success? (e.g., Upon teacher request, Joe will have one instance of "out of seat" behavior for 5 consecutive days.)

    Arrive on time for class daily for 2 consecutive weeks _____

    No rude/inappropriate verbal comments when given an assignment in any class for 2 consecutive weeks _____

    Pants on waist for 2 consecutive weeks _____

  4. Maintenance (fade reinforcers and prompting)

    Daily verbal prompts fade to every other class, then once a day, then every other day_____

  5. Home/School Coordination Plan

    Parents contacted when Jerry has a good day _____

  6. Implementers (Provide a copy of this plan to all implementers and list date received by implementers.)

    OHI teacher _____

    Individual aide _____

    General education teachers _____

  7. Additional support needed (e.g., staff training, budget for rewards, teacher release time) _____

  8. Will the student follow school rules as stated in the handbook?
    _X_ yes ___ no

(continued)

List exceptions:

_____

_____

C. Behavior Intervention Plan Progress Monitoring

First Quarter Review	Third Quarter Review
Second Quarter Review	Fourth Quarter Review

Please attach any behavioral contracts to the plan.

Case Study Framework Questions

1. What makes this a contemplation case?
2. How do emotions influence behaviors in the main characters?
3. How is the factual information consistent with current professional literature?
4. Are issues oversimplified? If so, how?
5. Are people stereotyped? If so, how?
6. Discuss teacher dispositions that could facilitate interaction (i.e., self-reflection, tolerance for others, collaboration, multiple perspectives, sound ethical judgment, motivation to work with students with a variety of needs, capacity for advocacy) or that could become a barrier to working with the student discussed in this case.

Thinking Critically About the Case

1. Describe Jerry's behavior in and out of the classroom.
2. What strengths does Jerry exhibit?
3. To what extent is each person's perspective reflected in the behavior intervention plan?
4. If you were the general education English teacher, how would you accommodate Jerry?
5. As the general education teacher, what responsibilities do you have as outlined in the Behavior Intervention Plan?
6. What other professionals should be involved, and what should they be doing?

Activity

Based on your review of the case information presented, rewrite several portions of the Behavior Intervention Plan.

1. Describe one target (a target behavior can be positive, or something you want the student to do or negative, something you want to eliminate) behavior that should be addressed (write an objective description).
2. Describe the desired behavior that should replace the target behavior (write an objective description in measurable terms).
3. Create at least three interventions to replace the target behavior with the desired behavior.
4. What should happen if the desired behavior occurs? (State types of reinforcements and schedule.)
5. What happens if the desired behavior does not occur? (Include consequences and prompting.)
6. What are the criteria for success?
7. How will the desired behavior be maintained (e.g., through fade reinforcements and prompting)?
8. How will the home and school coordinate this plan?
9. Who will implement this plan?
10. What additional support is needed?

RESOURCES FOR FURTHER INVESTIGATION

Print

Minskoff, E., & Allsopp, D. (2002). *Academic success strategies for adolescents with learning disabilities and ADHD*. Baltimore: Paul H. Brookes.

Sholaman, S., & Scholzman. (2000). Chaos in the classroom: Looking at ADHD. *Educational Leadership, 58*(3), 28–33.

Turecki, S., & Tonner, L. (2000). *The difficult child*. New York: Bantam.

Web

Children and Adults with Attention-Deficit/Hyperactivity Disorder
http://www.chadd.org

National Attention Deficit Disorder Association
http://www.add.org/

Appendix

Individual Education Plan Drafting Activities and Templates

Activity

Several students in this text have been identified as having a disability and as needing special education and related services. Although forms for Individual Education Plans (IEPs) vary and the law detailing exact components of the IEP changes, it is useful to think critically about the individual needs of the student. On the next few pages, you will find blank forms for the following pieces of an IEP.

- Current Levels of Performance and Goals
- General Education Modifications/Adaptations/Supplemental Aids and Services and/or Supports for School Personnel; Special Education and Related Services
- Transition Plan (for students age 14 and over)
- Participation in State and Local Assessments

As you reflect on the case studies, you may want to form mock IEP teams for a particular case. Each person should assume an appropriate role (e.g., parent, special education teacher). In a role-play, you will then discuss the specific needs of the student in the case and complete appropriate pieces of the IEP. Note that all pieces will not be appropriate for all students. For example, if the student is ten years old, transition is not likely to be completed. If the student is three years old, participation in state and local assessments would not be completed.

CURRENT LEVELS OF PERFORMANCE AND GOALS

Current Performance Levels: Descriptive statements of all areas that are impacted by the student's disability. What is the student able to do and where are the areas of concern? Includes how the student's disability affects his/her involvement and progress in the general education curriculum.

1. Academic:

2. Social/Emotional:

3. Independent Functioning:

4. Speech/Language/Communication:

5. Vocational Skills:

6. Motor Skills:

7. Other:

Annual Goals: Must be measurable and address meeting the student's needs that result from the disability to enable him/her to be involved and progress in the general curriculum. What do we want the student to be able to do?

Goal Type: __ Annual __ Transition

Goal Statement: _____

_____

Implementer: _____ **Projected Completion Date:** _____

Monitoring Schedule	Evaluation Procedures	Criteria for Mastery
__ Daily	__ Tests	__ 71–81% Accuracy
__ Weekly	__ Charting	__ 81–90% Accuracy
__ Monthly	__ Observations	__ 91–100% Accuracy
__ Quarterly	__ Daily Log	__ of ____ Trials
__ Grade period	__ Other _____	__ Other _____
__ Other _____		

Goal Type: __ **Annual** __ **Transition**

Goal Statement: _____

_____

Implementer: _____ **Projected Completion Date:** _____

Monitoring Schedule	Evaluation Procedures	Criteria for Mastery
__ Daily	__ Tests	__ 71–81% Accuracy
__ Weekly	__ Charting	__ 81–90% Accuracy
__ Monthly	__ Observations	__ 91–100% Accuracy
__ Quarterly	__ Daily Log	__ of ____ Trials
__ Grade period	__ Other _____	__ Other _____
__ Other _____		

Goal Type: __ **Annual** __ **Transition**

Goal Statement: _____

_____

Implementer: _____ **Projected Completion Date:** _____

Monitoring Schedule	Evaluation Procedures	Criteria for Mastery
__ Daily	__ Tests	__ 71–81% Accuracy
__ Weekly	__ Charting	__ 81–90% Accuracy
__ Monthly	__ Observations	__ 91–100% Accuracy
__ Quarterly	__ Daily Log	__ of ____ Trials
__ Grade period	__ Other _____	__ Other _____
__ Other _____		

General Education Modifications/Adaptations/Supplemental Aids and Services and/or Supports for School Personnel; Special Education and Related Services		
Subject Area (Academic and Nonacademic)	**Explanation of General Education Modifications/ Adaptations/Supplemental Aids and Services and/or Supports for School Personnel**	**Special Education Support Necessary?(Yes/No) If Yes, Specify**

Needed Service: Special Education or Related Service	**Location of Service (General or Special Education or Other)**	**Minutes per Day**	**Date of Initiation Services**	**Anticipated Duration**	**Frequency of Service**

TRANSITION PLAN

Post-School Vision (include employment, education, and living arrangements): _____

_____

Course of Study: Year 1_____

Year 2_____

Year 3_____

Year 4_____

Other_____

Annual Needed Services (school, community, and agency services for the next school year in order for this student to progress toward his/her post-school vision):

Instruction: __ Yes __ No

_____

Community Experiences: __ Yes __ No

_____

Employment and other post-school adult living objectives: __ Yes __ No

_____

As appropriate, daily living skills and functional vocational evaluation: __ Yes__ No

_____

If appropriate, a statement of each outside agency's responsibilities, or linkage before the student leaves the school setting:

_____

_____

_____

PARTICIPATION IN STATE AND LOCAL ASSESSMENTS

Grade Placement of Student: _____

The student will:

__ Participate in the entire State assessment with no accommodations

__ Participate in the entire State assessment with accommodations

__ Participate in part(s) of the State assessment (specified below)

__ NOT participate in the State assessment

__ Participate in the entire district-wide assessment with no accommodations

__ Participate in the entire district-wide assessment with accommodations

__ Participate in part(s) of the district-wide assessment (specified below)

__ NOT participate in the district-wide assessment

If the student is completing the assessment(s) with accommodations, specify the needed accommodations (e.g., extended time, alternate setting)

If the student will not participate in part or all of the assessment(s), specify why the assessment is not appropriate and document the alternate assessment to be given, including any needed accommodations.